Where does Luisa's passion for cooking come from?

Luisa grew up in a traditional Italian family, in which cooking was integral to family life. Many of Luisa's favorite recipes in *Spices of Life and Herbs, Too!* are Italian, several learned from her mother or from one of her many aunts.

Her career as an interior designer took her to Thailand in her twenties, where she was the only European working in one of Southeast Asia's top architectural and design firms. She lived with a Thai family, learned the language, and was rapidly shopping at the local market, being taught how to cook dozens of different dishes by incredibly helpful Thai friends and stall-keepers. So, again, it's no surprise that many of the recipes in *Spices of Life and Herbs, Too!* have a Southeast Asian touch, or in several cases are authentic Thai recipes.

Luisa's life and career then took her to Switzerland, where the cuisine is a kind of high-quality European fusion; and also where she learned to cook the perfect rösti. And it was in Switzerland where she met her English, Yorkshire pudding-loving husband. So, a few recipes for roasts have crept into *Spices of Life and Herbs, Too!*

Luisa and her husband now divide their time between Switzerland and London, which is where she has come to share her husband's taste for Indian cuisine. Never having visited India herself, she has nevertheless become fascinated by the London Indian restaurant culture, especially the 'From Bombay with Love' theme epitomized by the innovative Dishoom restaurants which present Bombay street food to a discerning British public. She has experimented with several of these ideas. So you'll find some Indian recipes in *Spices of Life and Herbs, Too!*, too. Unsurprising, given the title!

Demonstrations and Social Media

Cooking demonstrations of some of the dishes in *Spices of Life and Herbs, Too!* are available on Luisa's YouTube channel: lockedintastes.

And you can follow Luisa and Locked-in-Tastes on Instagram: @lockedintastes.

Luisa hopes that you find something spicy which appeals to your tastes!

SPICES OF LIFE
AND HERBS, TOO!

Recipes with Locked-in Tastes

Luisa Fortunato

AUSTIN MACAULEY PUBLISHERS
LONDON • CAMBRIDGE • NEW YORK • SHARJAH

Copyright © Luisa Fortunato 2023

All rights reserved. No part of this publication may be reproduced, distributed, or transmitted in any form or by any means, including photocopying, recording, or other electronic or mechanical methods, without the prior written permission of the publisher, except in the case of brief quotations embodied in critical reviews and certain other non-commercial uses permitted by copyright law. For permission requests, write to the publisher.

Any person who commits any unauthorized act in relation to this publication may be liable to criminal prosecution and civil claims for damages.

Ordering Information
Quantity sales: Special discounts are available on quantity purchases by corporations, associations, and others. For details, contact the publisher at the address below.

Publisher's Cataloging-in-Publication data
Fortunato, Luisa
Spices of Life and Herbs, Too!

ISBN 9781638291770 (Paperback)
ISBN 9798891559998 (Hardback)
ISBN 9781638291787 (ePub e-book)

Library of Congress Control Number: 2023904303

www.austinmacauley.com/us

First Published 2023
Austin Macauley Publishers LLC
40 Wall Street, 33rd Floor, Suite 3302
New York, NY 10005
USA

mail-usa@austinmacauley.com
+1 (646) 5125767

This book is dedicated to the great female chefs: Julia Childs, Marcella Hazan, Susanna Foo, and Anne-Sophie Pic. These talented women have inspired, guided, and taught me, through their words, how to reach for the stars.

Spices and Herbs: What's the Difference?

Spices and herbs are often lumped together, almost in a single word, 'herbs and spices.' But what's the difference?

Spices are hot and spicy, and herbs are, well, herby, right?

Not exactly. Strictly speaking, a spice comes from the seeds of a plant, whereas herbs come from the leaves or occasionally the root. So juniper, vanilla, coffee, and chocolate, on this definition, are spices, but not spicy, whereas curry leaves and ginger, though quite spicy, are herbs.

All this is a good reason for abandoning the distinction. What we need is a single word for the category. In fact, when I was young, my Italian parents in America used the word 'spice' to cover the lot. That's why this book is called 'Spices of Life' with the sub-line 'and Herbs, too!' for the benefit of any pedantic readers.

Locked-in Tastes

My first venture into publishing was Locked-in Tastes – Culinary Adventures under lockdown, an e-book which raised 120% of its target in donations for charity.

At the time of writing it, over three billion people were in lockdown: more than a third of the world's population.

But only some of the recipes in Locked-in Tastes were mine. Most of the sixty recipes were contributed by ordinary people from over a dozen countries around the world under lockdown, in the hope that their recipes might help others in lockdown. Locked-in Tastes is still available and can be downloaded, free, from our website: www.lockedintastes.com.

This new book, Spices of Life, comprises eighty-seven of my own favourite recipes, all involving a spice or a herb (or many). It's the book I've always wanted to write.

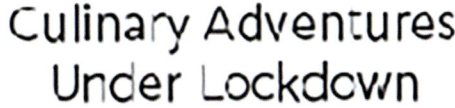

LOCKED-IN TASTES

Culinary Adventures Under Lockdown

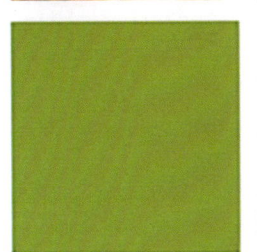

My 'Alphabet' of Spices and Herbs

Allspice – also known as Бахар (Bahar) in Bulgarian, Ziele angielskie in Polish, Nové koření in Czech, Yeni Bahar in Turkish and Krydpeppar in Swedish. It comes from the berries of Pimenta dioica, a mid-canopy tree native to the Greater Antilles, Southern Mexico, Central America, and Jamaica. It has the aroma of a blend of cinnamon, cloves, and nutmeg. Whole allspice is used mainly in pickling, and ground allspice is used in savoury dishes, baked goods, puddings, and preserves.

Aniseed – originated in the Middle East, where it is grown today as a commercial crop. Small white flowers bloom in mid-summer, followed by tiny liquor-ice-flavoured fruits called aniseed. Aniseed adds rich flavour to biscuits, cakes, candies, bread, and applesauce.

Basil – sweet, sweet basil, to Italians, is a symbol of love. What most of us adore is basil's pungent, spicy-clove flavour and aroma. Shred its leaves and breathe deeply; its pungent smell permeates.

Bay Leaf – (laurus nobilis, lauraceae) often used to give soups, stews, braises, and curries a distinctive flavour and fragrance. It's best to remove the leaves before serving.

Capers – what is a caper? They are the flower buds of a small bush found in Mediterranean countries. These buds are dried and then pickled in vinegar with some salt. To reduce saltiness (but why?), rinse before using. The piquant taste of capers penetrates quickly. I ask: What would vitello tonnato be without capers?

Cardamom – is a member of the ginger or zingiberaceae (love that crazy name) family and is one of the most expensive of spices. It comes from

Southeast India and is widely used not only throughout Asia but also in many Scandinavian dishes. Who knew?

Chili Powder – Chili peppers (which can be spelled chilli or chili), from which chili powder is made, have been a part of the human diet since at least 7500 BC and were cultivated around the globe after Columbus's time. Scientific studies are investigating capsaicin, the compound that gives red pepper its heat, which may inhibit the growth of fat cells – if true, it kind of makes you want to eat a handful every day.

Chocolate – Cocoa has been cultivated for at least three millennia in Central America and Mexico, with its earliest documented use around 1100 BC. This famous aphrodisiac has inspired lovers, writers, chefs, and sweethearts to create imaginative tastes and shapes. The cocoa seeds are roasted, husked, and ground, often sweetened and saturated with vanilla – thank you, Côte d'Ivoire.

Cinnamon – is available powdered or in sticks. It is a member of the laurel or lauraceae family and grows on the island of Sri Lanka and along the southwestern coast of India. The inner bark of the tree yields the 'bark cinnamon' sold in scroll-like sticks. Break these scrolls into as small pieces as possible and then grind them in a spice mill. Their aroma is positively hypnotic.

Cloves – are the unopened flower bud of a tree that grows in many of the warmer regions of the world, such as India, Malaysia, the Philippines, Sumatra, and Brazil. Cloves may be purchased either whole or ground and have an enchanting pungent aroma. Remember: less is more.

Coffee – essential to tiramisu and many early morning routines!

Coriander – is an annual herb in the family apiaceae. Coriander (also called cilantro) has thin, rounded, tooth-like bright green leaves resembling flat-leaf parsley and is also called fresh coriander or Chinese parsley. It is tangy with citrus accents and is a secret ingredient in most Asian cuisine.

Cumin – has been in use since ancient times. Seeds excavated at the south

Iraqi site Tel ed-Der have been dated to the second millennium BC. Cumin, ground or used as whole seeds, adds an earthy and warming feeling to food, making it a staple in certain stews and soups as well as spiced sauces such as chili gravy.

Curry Leaves – (Murraya koenigii, or curry leaf tree) is a tropical to sub-tropical tree in the family rutaceae and is native to India. Besides being packed with carbohydrates, fiber, calcium, phosphorous, iron, and vitamins such as Vitamin C, Vitamin A, Vitamin B, and Vitamin E, curry leaves add a specific Indian touch to dishes and are believed to help heart function and fight infections.

Curry Powder – the basis of Indian cooking. Curry powder includes turmeric, ginger, mustard seeds, fenugreek, coriander, cinnamon, cayenne pepper and cardamom and brings a range of health benefits. It is anti-inflammatory, anti-oxidant, and aids cholesterol and blood sugar levels. The turmeric gives curry powder its bright yellow punch!

Dill – one of the oldest herbs. It is a native of Southern Europe and Western Asia. It has tender, feathery, blue-green fronds branching off a central stem. Both seeds and leaves have a sharp, slightly absinthian taste.

Fenugreek – is an ancient spice which has been in use since the Iron Age and is an invaluable ingredient in Mediterranean, Middle Eastern and Southeast Asian cuisine. Fenugreek leaves, seeds, oil, or powder all add a fresh taste.

Five-Spice Powder – is an essential ingredient in Chinese and Vietnamese cuisine. In spite of its name, five-spice powder actually incorporates up to seven components: ground star anise, cinnamon, nutmeg, black pepper, and ginger as well as fennel and cloves.

Galangal – is a rhizome of any of four plant species in the ginger family. Available in most Asian markets, it comes dried, as a powder, in a paste, or (preferably) fresh. It is essential in Southeast Asian soups and curries. It is also believed to have medicinal value in promoting digestion and easing respiratory diseases and stomach conditions.

Garam Masala – comes from North India where it is home-ground from three to eight of the spices known as 'warm' spices in the Ayur Veda book of medicine. These are dried chilies, black peppercorns, cinnamon, mace, nutmeg, cloves, coriander seeds, and cumin seeds.

Ginger – is a warming herb with a pungent aroma and flavour. It enhances all kinds of foods, from confectionery and cakes to savoury dishes. It is widely used in the cuisines of the Far East, especially in curries and stir-fries.

Grenadine – a non-alcoholic syrup used to flavour and colour cocktails and cold drinks. Containing pomegranate, lemon juice, and sugar, it is a colourful way to sweeten your favourite gin.

Herbs of Provence – is a classic herb blend using fresh or dried herbs. Very popular in the South of France, it is used to season everything from soups to grilled chicken. The traditional version uses lavender: soooo provençale (and we love Provence!).

Juniper Berries – Used particularly in European cuisine, they are not a berry as the name suggests but a cone (a female cone, in fact) and is the only spice derived from conifers. They are also famous for giving gin its distinctive flavour.

Kaffir Lime Leaves – Found in Asian markets, they are thick, dark green, and shiny on top but porous and pale underneath. Tear a leaf to smell the distinct aroma. These leaves add the quintessential flavour to Thai and Southeast Asian cuisine. Add to curries and soups to taste the real Thailand. Don't even think of preparing a Tom Yam without them.

Lavender – During Roman times, lavender flowers were sold for hundred denarii per pound, which was about the same as a month's wages for a farm labourer or fifty haircuts from the local barber. Lavender was commonly used in Roman baths to scent the water, and it was thought to restore the skin. Today, lavender is mostly used in desserts and in tea, but it also lends its smoky, floral essence to meats, fish, seafood, and roasted vegetables.

Lemongrass – Ah! This fragrant herb that looks like a petrified scallion is a versatile one. It is widely used as a flavouring ingredient in Southeast Asian dishes. There are more than fifty species in this collection of scented grasses.

Linden Leaves – (or tirol Tea, tilia platyphyllos) is a species of flowering plant in the family malvaceae. It is a deciduous tree, native to much of Europe, growing on lime-rich soils. Linden flowers are used to treat colds, cough, fever, infections, inflammation, and high blood pressure as well as a diuretic, antispasmodic, and sedative. The flowers were added to baths to quell hysteria and steeped to make a tea to relieve anxiety-related indigestion and irregular heartbeat.

Marjoram – is an aromatic herb in the mint (lamiaceae) family that has been cultivated for thousands of years. In Greek mythology, marjoram was grown by the Goddess Aphrodite. Native to the Mediterranean, North Africa, and Western Asia, marjoram is often called sweet marjoram to distinguish it from oregano varieties such as wild marjoram (origanum vulgare) and pot marjoram (origanum onites), also known as Turkish oregano.

Mint – spearmint, lemon-mint, or peppermint. It is said that mint is the most popular flavouring in the world, appearing in so many foodstuffs and medicines that is seems almost ordinary. "Woe unto you, scribes and Pharisees, hypocrites! For ye pay tithe of mint and anise and cumin and have omitted the weightier [matters] of the law, judgment, mercy, and faith: these ought ye to have done and not to leave the other undone." (Mathew 23:23)

Mustard Seeds – are tiny seeds from three different varieties of the mustard plant: black mustard (brassica nigra), brown Indian mustard (B. juncea), or white/yellow mustard (B. hirta/sinapis alba). Crush into a powder. Add salt and white pepper and a bit of vinegar – et violà, you have prepared fresh mustard.

Nigella Seeds – (N. sativa), also commonly known as black cumin, are used throughout Mediterranean, Middle-Eastern, Indian, and Polish cuisine. One wonders how this little seed can add such punch.

Nutmeg – is the egg-shaped seed of the myristica fragrans tree, indigenous to the Banda Islands, now part of Indonesia. Indeed the Banda Islands, once controlled by the British but coveted by the Dutch (who adore nutmeg to this day), were the world's only source of nutmeg and also of mace, the dried reddish covering of the nutmeg seed. History buffs may recall that Henry Hudson, working for the Dutch Trading Company, raced across the Atlantic searching for a quicker route to the Spice Islands and by chance discovered Manhattan, which he claimed for the Dutch. To make a long story short, Manhattan was then swapped for the Banda Islands, with the British taking control of the whole Hudson River area, whilst the Dutch gained a monopoly supply of their beloved nutmeg from the Banda Islands.

Orange Blossom Water – a pleasant surprise in many Mediterranean and Middle-Eastern desserts. One sniff and you are transported into a delicate orange grove. In Lebanon, it is added to boiling water to create a digestif known as white coffee and finishes off a feast with a pleasant surprise. In India, orange blossom water pops up in many traditional desserts.

Oregano – also called wild marjoram: similar to sweet marjoram but bushier and more spreading. Oregano is very assertive and peppery with hints of pine. Chop the leaves roughly or finely and add early in cooking. Oregano is best known as the 'pizza herb.'

Pandam Leaves – (pandanus amaryllifolius)

Grown in most households in Sri Lanka and essential throughout Southeast Asia, these leaves are used widely to sweeten cakes (steeping the leaves in coconut milk) or wrapping them around meat or fish on the BBQ to keep the food moist. They add a flowery flavour and, in baking, a marvellous green hue.

Paprika – is a spice made from the air-dried fruits of the chili pepper family of the species capsicum annuum. The use of paprika expanded from Iberia throughout Africa and Asia and ultimately reached Central Europe through the Balkans, which were under Ottoman rule, explaining the Hungarian origin of the modern English term. In Spanish, paprika has been known as pimentón since the 1500s when it became a typical ingredient across the western world.

Parsley – (petrosellinium crispum) is a delicate-tasting herb which is widely used in European, Middle-Eastern, and American cuisine. The curly variety is mostly for decoration, while the flat-leaf variety has more flavour.

Pepper – Pepper is the most popular spice in the world and comes in many varieties: black, white, pink, red, and green. For the most part, pepper is imported from India and Indonesia.

Poppy seed – (papaver somniferum) is an oilseed from the opium poppy. Traceable back to the ancient Egyptians, it is now a favourite ingredient in Central European cuisine, but common usage dates back to the Egyptians.

Rose – (rosa) Rosehips, rose petals, rose water, and rose syrup all come from this glorious flower of the perennial flowering plant, genus rosa, and turn any beverage or dessert into a Vitamin-C-packed experience fit for royalty.

Rosemary – (salvia rosmarinus) derived from Latin, ros marinus ('dew of the sea') is a perennial with tiny blue, pink, purple, or white flowers in the spring. Plant it in your garden and, if trimmed, you will enjoy the benefits for twenty-five to thirty years to come. Add it to soups, marinades, roasts, and focaccia and also to the baking tray when roasting potatoes to add a woody aroma and crunchy texture.

Saffron – belongs to the iridaceae family, which includes irises and crocuses. Saffron consists of the deep orange-coloured stamens of the crocus. It takes about thirty-five thousand flowers to produce a pound of saffron, making it the most expensive spice on the planet.

Sage – (salvia officinalis), also known as garden sage or common sage, is a perennial, evergreen subshrub with woody stems, greyish leaves, and blue to purplish flowers. It is a member of the family lamiaceae and is native to the Mediterranean region, though it has naturalised in many places throughout the world. It has a long history of medicinal and culinary use.

Salt – composed primarily of sodium chloride that is essential for animal life. There are forty-one verses which refer to salt in the English translation of the King James's Bible, the earliest being the story of Lot's wife, who was turned into a pillar of salt when she disobediently looked back at the wicked cities of Sodom and Gomorrah (Genesis 19:26). The Roman army was paid in salt and this is the origin of the word 'salary.' Mahatma Gandhi took a long parade called 'Dandi March' or 'Salt Sathya Graha' against taxes levied by the then British rulers. Salt is great; it brings out the flavours of foods and, although technically neither a herb nor a spice, usually only a pinch is needed.

Sesame Seeds – (sesamum indicum) are one of the oldest oilseed crops known, domesticated for over three thousand years. It has many species, most being wild and native to sub-Saharan Africa. It is a common ingredient around the globe due to its rich and nutty taste.

Star Anise – (illcium verum) is an evergreen tree native to Vietnam and Southwest China. The star-shaped seed resembles aniseed but in fact is not related to it. It's commonly used in Chinese, Indonesian, and Indian cuisine. It is also an important component of five-spice powder. Star Anise spice is also cultivated to produce shikimic acid which is used in pharmaceutical products such as Tami flu, which seemed to help to combat the swine-flu pandemic in 2009 and also E-coli outbreaks.

Sumac – Nicknamed – The Spice of Life: The word 'sumac' traces its etymology from the Arabic summāq (سماق) and from Syriac summāq (محمص) – meaning 'red.' The fruits of the genus rhus are ground into a reddish-purple powder used as a spice in Middle Eastern cuisine to add a lemony taste to salads or meat in Arab cuisine.

Tamarind – (tamarindus indica) A tropical tree that produces a pod-like fruit. Crack open its shell and eat the sweet/sour fruit directly from the pod, being mindful of the stones inside. As a pulp, tamarind is used in abundance in Indian curries and is added to chutneys and sauces.

Thai Basil – sometimes called anise basil or liquor-ice basil. Because it has an aniseed or liquor-ice-like scent and taste, Thai Basil is different from the western varieties and one should not be substituted for the other. Thai basil has thin, pointy, purple and green leaves and instantly transforms a salad or main dish into a quick trip to Southeast Asia!

Thyme – clusters of tiny green leaves on a thin, woody stem. The most common variety for cooking is English thyme. Other varieties include lemon thyme and caraway thyme. Thyme has a subtle pine, lemon, and spicy flavour.

It is versatile and widely complementary to many dishes but can overwhelm delicate foods. Use liberally but carefully.

Turmeric – has a musky, peppery flavour. It is used mainly in ground form to colour foods yellow, especially Indian curries and soups. Use sparingly as an alternative to saffron.

Vanilla – climbing orchid of the genus vanilla, esp. V. planifolia, its name derives from the Spanish word 'vainilla' or little pod. The plant bears pod-like fruit, yielding an extract used in flavouring for ice cream and also in perfume.

Violette – sometimes called crème de violette or liqueur de violette is made from violet flowers (viola species) and adds that soft violet hue to cocktails, desserts, and confections. It's truly a taste of spring!

The Recipes

The recipes which follow in this cookbook are in alphabetical order of the main spice or herb featured. Below, for ease of search, the recipes are grouped by category with recipe numbers.

Starters and Snacks

Gazpacho: **Recipe 14**

Curry sauce for ravioli: **Recipe 26**

Tom kha goong – Thai prawn soup and coconut milk: **Recipe 30**

Poached peaches + ricotta buttercream + crunchy panko topping: **Recipe 33**

Thai Moo sarong – pork wrapped in golden threads: **Recipe 34**

Yam wun sen – seafood and cellophane Thai noodle salad: **Recipe 41**

Raita: **Recipe 50**

Chestnut gnocchi with gorgonzola and pear: **Recipe 51**

Carciofi alla Romana – Artichokes Roman-style: **Recipe 60**

Salad of cherry tomatoes, fraises des bois, mesclun, and parmesan: **Recipe 62**

Cacio e pepe con tagliolini: **Recipe 61**

Rosemary focaccia: **Recipe 66**

Risotto alla Milanese with lemon: **Recipe 69**

(also see our lockedintastes YouTube video)

Stuffed zucchini flowers: **Recipe 70** (also see our **lockedintastes**

YouTube video)

Salad Olivieh: **Recipe 77**

Grilled aubergine with turmeric, chili, and pomegranate seeds: **Recipe 83**

Insalata di pomodori con burrata + basilico: **Recipe 6**

Main Courses

Jamaican jerk chicken: **Recipe 3**

Perfect roast beef: **Recipe 9**

Vitello tonnato: **Recipe 10** (also see our lockedintastes YouTube video)

Lemon sole with caper sauce: **Recipe 11**

Tandoori chicken: **Recipe 13**

Roast gammon with mango chutney glaze: **Recipe 19**

Scallopini alla Milanese with chicken: **Recipe 25**

Murgh Makhani – Indian butter chicken: **Recipe 29**

Sweet and sour prawns: **Recipe 2**

Gaeng keow waan gai – Thai green curry with chicken: **Recipe 31**

Chicken tikka: **Recipe 32**

Roast whole chicken: **Recipe 39**

Roast rack of lamb: **Recipe 56**

Baked aubergine with tomatoes and feta: **Recipe 55**

Whole sea bass baked in salted crust: **Recipe 72**

Roast pork with perfect crackling: **Recipe 71**

Chinese lemon chicken: **Recipe 73**

Teriyaki salmon: **Recipe 74**

Spicy grilled beef filet: **Recipe 75**

Roast quail with tamarind and orange glaze: **Recipe 78**

Pad krapao: **Recipe 79** (also see our lockedintastes YouTube video)

Gaeng pet ped yang – Thai red curry with duck breast: **Recipe 80**

Stuffed peppers in a mascarpone tomato sauce: **Recipe 82**

Polenta with roasted mushrooms and thyme: **Recipe 81**

Roast pumpkin and chickpea salad with coriander dressing: **Recipe 22**

Lonza di maiale alle nocciole – Pork loin with hazelnut sauce: **Recipe 67**

Gai Yang – Grilled North-Eastern-style Thai chicken: **Recipe 21**

Tandoori lamb chops: **Recipe 24**

Sides and Sauces

Pesto alla Genovese: **Recipe 7** (also see our lockedintastes YouTube video)

Basil oil: **Recipe 5**

Salsa rossa estiva: **Recipe 8** (also see our lockedintastes YouTube video)

Roasted cauliflower with chili: **Recipe 15**

Sautéed green beans with vanilla salt and butter: **Recipe 85**

Grilled Mediterranean vegetables with lemon-infused olive oil: **Recipe 76**

Chinese plum sauce: **Recipe 1**

Versatile spicy Thai savoury sauce: **Recipe 36**

(also see our lockedintastes YouTube video)

Thai sweet chili sauce: **Recipe 35**

Sweet sautéed carrots with orange and marjoram: **Recipe 45**

Piquant potatoes: **Recipe 48** (also see our lockedintastes YouTube video)

Sandra's roasted potatoes: **Recipe 59**

(also see our lockedintastes YouTube video)

Gratinato di finocchio con noce moscata: **Recipe 52**

Mango chutney: **Recipe 49**

Sicilian blood orange and fennel salad: **Recipe 53**

Saffron chili butter: **Recipe 68**

Pandan juice: **Recipe 57**

Moroccan-style couscous: **Recipe 23**

Cucumber and dill salad: **Recipe 27**

Desserts and Sweet Snacks

Italian Aniseed Biscuits: **Recipe 4**

Peach crumble with cardamom crust: **Recipe 12**

Flourless chocolate cake: **Recipe 16**

Luisa's banana bread: **Recipe 18**

Forest-fruit clafoutis: **Recipe 17**

Tiramisu: **Recipe 20**

Lemon madeleines with lavender: **Recipe 42**

Orange and pineapple salad with mint sugar: **Recipe 47**

Pandan coconut ice cream: **Recipe 58**

Lemon poppy-seed fairy cakes: **Recipe 63**

Rose and pomegranate ice cream: **Recipe 65**

Vanilla crème brûlée: **Recipe 84**

Salzburger Nockerl: **Recipe 86**

Drinks and Cocktails

Gimme a gimlet, please! **Recipe 28**

Singapore sling: **Recipe 38**

A Swiss Kiss: **Recipe 37 (also see our lockedintastes YouTube video)**

The Remedy – G and T: **Recipe 40**

Nam manao – limeade with lemongrass: **Recipe 43**

Mojito: **Recipe 46**

Ramos Gin Fizz: **Recipe 54**

Duchess of Cambridge cocktail: **Recipe 64**

Linden leaf tea: **Recipe 44**

Aviation cocktail: **Recipe 87**

5-Spice powder

Recipe 1

Chinese Plum Sauce

Why not make your own sauce using fresh plums from the market rather than the industrial bottled supermarket version? It's easy and here's how!

Sauce
Makes 3 to 4 jars
Prep time: 10 minutes
Cooking time: 30 minutes
Sterilising time: 15 minutes
Gluten-free

Ingredients

1kg/2.25lbs plums, pitted and chopped
1 small onion, chopped
60 ml/2fl oz. cider vinegar
500 g/1lb jam sugar
60 ml/2fl oz. soy sauce
3 tbs honey
4 tbs grated fresh ginger
3 tbs Chinese five-spice powder
4 cinnamon sticks
4 star anises
8 cloves
4 sterilised number 10 size jars (300ml/10 ounces)

Method

Place all ingredients except for the spices in a medium-sized saucepan and bring to the boil. Reduce the heat and simmer uncovered for 30 minutes. Use a handheld mixer to make a very smooth purée.

Now add the five-spice powder to the plum purée and simmer uncovered for 30 minutes until the purée is nice and thick.

In each of the sterilised jars, place 1 cinnamon stick, 1 star anise, and 2 cloves. Ladle the hot plum sauce into the jars, filling them almost to the very top. Seal tight and place the jars in boiling water to sterilise for 15 minutes.

Remove the jars from the HOT water. Test to make certain that the lid is nice and tight and then cool.

Label the jars. The plum sauce can be stored for up to one year.

5-Spice powder

Recipe 2

Sweet and Sour Prawns

Sweet, sour, and always satisfying. Or substitute sliced pork loin, chicken, or for a vegetarian version, sliced tofu.

Main course
Serves 4
Prep Time: 10 mins
Cooking Time: 20 mins
Gluten-free

Ingredients

500g/1lb peeled and deveined prawns
Drizzle of vegetable oil
150g/5 oz. brown sugar
60ml/2fl oz. pineapple juice from can
of pineapple chunks
75ml/2.5fl oz. white vinegar
125ml/4fl oz. tomato concentrate
3tbs soy sauce
Splash of white wine
2tbs five-spice powder 200g/1 cup canned pineapple chunks, drained
(Keep juice for the sauce.)
1 red bell pepper seeded and cut into chunks
1 yellow bell pepper seeded and cut into chunks
6 spring onions cut into slices
Toasted cashews (generous)
Generous amount of dried Chinese
red chilies
Sprigs of fresh coriander

Method

   Over medium heat, add a drizzle of vegetable oil to the skillet or wok and then the bell peppers and cook for 4 to 5 minutes. Add the prawns and cook for 2 minutes. Then add the spring onions and pineapple chunks and stir.
   In a bowl, combine the sugar, pineapple juice, vinegar, tomato concentrate, and soy sauce. Stir until the sugar is dissolved. Pour the sauce into the skillet

or wok. Stir to coat the prawns, peppers, and spring onions. Bring to the boil. Then reduce heat to medium and simmer for 10 minutes, stirring a couple of times.

To serve:

On top, sprinkle the toasted cashews, dried red chilies and add the sprigs of fresh coriander. Serve immediately with steamed jasmine rice.

Allspice

Recipe 3

Jamaican Jerk Chicken

The secret of this fiery dish is to use freshly ground spices.

Main Course
Serves 8
Cooking time: 30 minutes
Marinating time: 9 hours
Gluten-free
Dairy-free

Ingredients

2 medium-sized chickens, quartered
1 onion, chopped
4 green onions, sliced
4 Scotch bonnet chilies, seeds discarded and chopped
1tbs five-spice powder
1tbs allspice berries, ground
3tbs black peppercorn
2tsp dried thyme, crumbled
1tsp freshly grated nutmeg
1tsp salt
175ml/3/4 cup soy sauce
1tbs olive oil
2 limes quartered for serving
Sprigs of fresh coriander

Method

For the marinade:

In a mortar and pestle, grind the allspice and black peppercorns. Add the crumbled thyme and freshly grated nutmeg. Then add the five-spice powder and salt. Pound until well combined.

Add the onion, green onions, and chilies and pound into a thick paste. Add the soy sauce and olive oil and stir.

Place the marinade into a plastic re-sealable bag. Add the chicken pieces and place into the refrigerator to marinate overnight.

Grill the chicken pieces on a BBQ or in the oven (medium to hot), turning occasionally until cooked: approx. 35 minutes.

Serve with the lime wedges and fresh sprigs of coriander, steamed rice, and your favourite summer salads.

Aniseed

Recipe 4

Italian Aniseed Biscuits

No celebration is complete without these biscuits!

Snack
Yields 40 biscuits
Prep time: 10 minutes
Cooking time: 10 to 12 minutes

Ingredients

165g/6 oz. unsalted butter
165g/6 oz. flour
100g/4 oz. corn flour (sifted)
90g/3 oz. icing sugar
1 egg
1tsp vanilla extract
1tsp aniseeds

Method

Preheat oven on 180°C/350F.
With an electric mixer, whip the butter and sugar for 10 minutes until it is very white in colour.
Add the egg, flour, corn flour, vanilla extract and aniseeds to make a dough.
Roll the dough out. Dust with flour.
Using a cookie cutter, cut into your desired shape. Place on a baking tray lined with baking paper.
Bake for 10 to 12 minutes.
When cool, decorate with icing sugar.

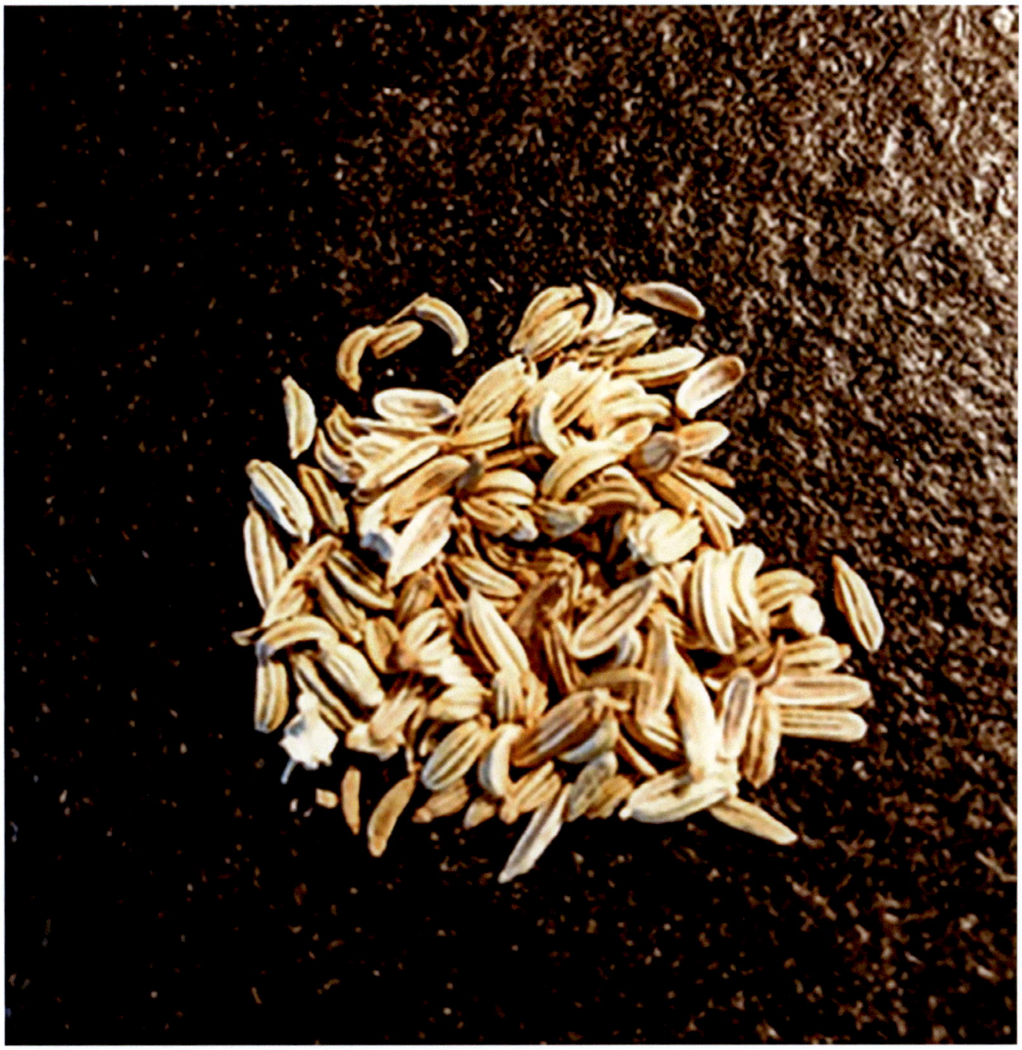

Basil

Recipe 5

Basil Oil

Even if you have no fresh basil, you can easily enjoy its fresh taste whenever and wherever you feel like it.

Sauce
Serves 12
Prep time: 10 minutes

Ingredients

2 large bunches of fresh basil leaves, closely packed
250ml/1 cup extra virgin olive oil
1 tsp salt
Pinch of dried red chili pepper flakes

Method

Blanch the basil leaves in boiling water for 10 seconds and then chill in a bowl
of ice water to stop the cooking process.
Place the basil in a mini food processor and pulse a few times.
Add the olive oil to the food processor and blend until you have a smooth sauce.
Use immediately or refrigerate and use for up to 7 days.
The flavours will intensify over time.

Basil

Recipe 6

Insalata di Pomodori con Burrata + Basilico – Tomato Salad with Burrata and Basil

Use only the freshest ingredients in order to enjoy this flavourful salad to the fullest!

First course
Serves 2
Prep time: 10 minutes
Gluten-free

Ingredients

3 large beefsteak tomatoes, sliced
1 large burrata cheese, room temperature
1 bunch of fresh basil (small bright green leaves are best)
Generous drizzle of basil oil: from specialty shop, or make your own: (see previous recipe.)
Pinch of salt flakes
A generous amount of freshly ground black pepper

Method

On a serving plate, arrange the sliced tomatoes. Position the burrata cheese in the centre.

Place the bunch of basil leaves. Sprinkle the salt flakes and drizzle the basil oil on top.

Crack a generous amount of freshly ground black pepper over the salad and serve.

Basil

Recipe 7

Pesto alla Genovese

This is the real thing. Recipe shared by dear friends Alessandro and Giovanna, who know what they are talking about, as Genova is their home!

Sauce
Serves 12
Prep time: 10 minutes

Ingredients

1 bunch of basil, stems removed
1/2tsp of salt
2 cloves of garlic, peeled (optional)
10 to 15 pine nuts
50g/2 oz. pecorino cheese, finely grated
50g/2 oz. parmesan cheese, finely grated

Method

Wash and dry the basil leaves. Add a little salt, the garlic cloves, and the pine nuts. Pound in a mortar until all is well mashed and forms a thick paste.

Note: The traditional recipe includes garlic, but if you're not a fan, simply omit it.

Add the cheeses to the pesto and mix.

Serve on top of piping-hot pasta, or on fish, or as a sauce with a caprese salad.

Storage: you don't have to use the pesto immediately. It can be stored in a glass jar, filled to the top with extra-virgin olive oil (to preserve it from oxidation) and kept in the refrigerator.

Bayleaf

Recipe 8

Salsa Rossa Estiva (Summer Red Sauce)

This is an amazingly versatile sauce that bursts with summer flavours. Try as a dip with fried zucchini or fritto di mare (fried seafood). It also makes a delicious spread on hunks of toasted crusty bread served with an aperitivo. Or pour on top of ricotta gnocchi for a yummy first course.

Sauce
Serves 4
Prep time: 30 minutes
Also see video on my YouTube channel: lockedintastes

Ingredients

1tbs olive oil
1 medium onion, chopped
1 sprig fresh rosemary
2 bay leaves
1 sprig sage
8 leaves fresh basil
250g/1 cup crushed tomatoes
2 red peppers, peeled, seeded, and roasted

Method

Heat the olive oil over medium heat and sauté the onion. Tie the rosemary, bay leaves, and basil together with a string and add the bundle to the pan. Cook it, stirring for 3 to 4 minutes. Add the tomatoes and peppers and cook for 5 minutes. Simmer on low heat for another 20 minutes.

Remove the herb bundle. Make purée with a handheld blender/mixer until the sauce is very smooth.

Serve warm.

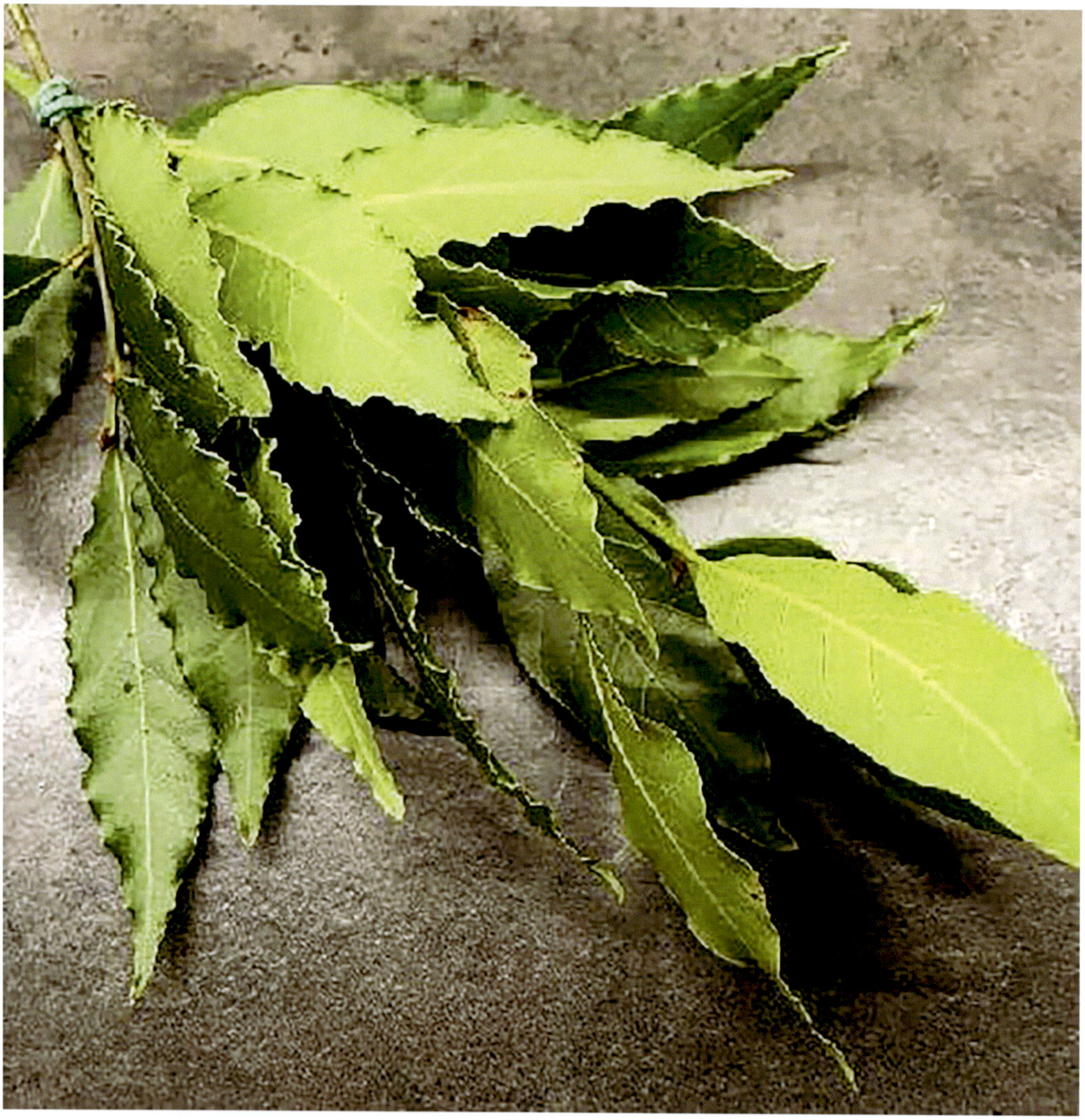

Bayleaf

Recipe 9

Perfect Roast Beef

Epitomises, the traditional Sunday lunch – just add roasted potatoes and Yorkshire pudding.

Photo: Alastair Douglas

Main course
Serves 6
Cooking time: 1 hour 5 minutes
Plus 15 minutes resting time
Gluten-free

Ingredients

1.5kg/3lbs of topside beef, room temperature
2 medium onions
2 celery stalks
1 bunch of fresh mixed herbs: bay leaf, thyme, rosemary, and sage
250ml/1 cup beef bouillon
Olive oil

Method

Preheat the oven 250°C/500°F
Wash and chop the vegetables (no need to peel) into a large roasting pan. Add the fresh herbs and drizzle with olive oil.
Pour the beef bouillon over the vegetables to prevent them from burning.
Place your joint on top of the herbs and vegetables. Drizzle the joint with olive oil and generously season with salt and pepper, making sure that the beef is well coated and the salt and pepper are rubbed into the meat.
Put the roasting pan into the oven and then turn the heat down to 200°C/400°F and cook for 1 hour for medium beef, 45 to 50 minutes for medium-rare, and 1 hour and 15 minutes for well-done.
Baste the beef halfway through cooking.
When the beef is cooked to your liking, take it out of the oven and place on a cutting board to rest for 15 minutes, covered with aluminium foil.
Serve with gravy, horseradish sauce, and/or mustard.

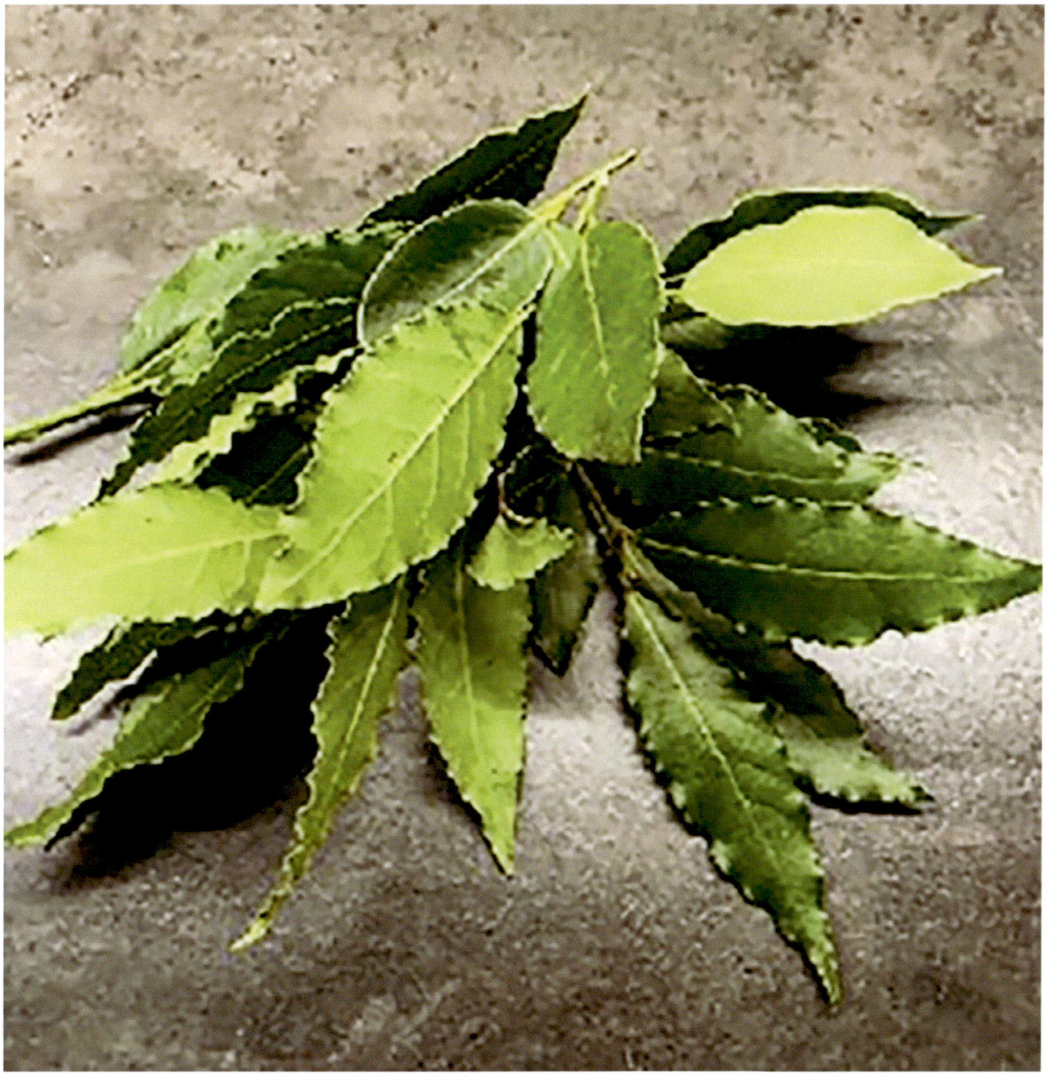

Capers

Recipe 10

Vitello Tonnato

A classic dish served cold. Super as a first course, for a buffet, or as a main course on a steamy day

Main course
Serves 4
Prep time: 20 minutes
Cooking time: 40 minutes
Chilling time: 1 hour

Also see video on my YouTube channel: lockedintastes

Ingredients

750gs/1.5lbs veal roast
125ml/half a cup vegetable bouillon
2 shallots, peeled and halved
1 carrot, chopped into chunks
1 bulb of fennel, chopped into chunks
2 sage leaves
2 sprigs of thyme
1 sprig of rosemary
1/2tsp salt

For the sauce

1 can albacore tuna in oil
125ml/half a cup plain full-fat yogurt
125ml/half a cup mayonnaise
60ml/quarter cup olive oil
60ml/quarter cup fresh lemon juice
2tbs of capers (I prefer big, fat ones.)

Method

Preheat the oven to 180°C/350ºF. In an ovenproof casserole with a lid, add a drizzle of olive oil, the chopped vegetables, and the bouillon. Place the roast on top. Add the herbs. Cover with the lid and roast for 35 to 40 minutes.

Remove from the oven. Place the roast on a cutting board. Cover with aluminium foil and allow to rest while you make the sauce.

Why not reserve the broth for a future use? It's great for risotto and soups.

For the Sauce

Combine the tuna, olive oil, yogurt, mayonnaise, and lemon juice in a mini food processor. Whip until smooth. Pour into a jug.

With a sharp carving knife, thinly slice the roast and place the slices flat on to a serving dish. Pour over the sauce. Sprinkle the lemon zest, capers, and a dash of paprika.

Chill for a least an hour to allow the flavours to combine. Serve with sprigs of chives.

Turkey breast can be substituted for veal. And if you are crazy about anchovies, add some!

Capers

Recipe 11

Lemon Sole with Caper Sauce

A lighter (and less pricey) version of Julia Child's Sole Meunière

Main course
Serves 2
Cooking time: 15 minutes

Ingredients

4 lemon sole filets
A pinch of sea salt
Freshly ground black pepper
2tbs unsalted butter
3tbs of extra virgin olive oil
1 shallot, minced
250ml/1 cup dry white wine
Juice from 1 lemon plus zest
2tbs of parsley, minced
2tbs of capers
100g/half a cup of flour (for dredging)

Method

Rinse the sole filets, pat them dry with kitchen towel, and then dredge in the flour and season with salt and pepper.

In a sauté pan, melt the butter and add the olive oil. Cook the filets on one side for 4 minutes and then flip and cook for a further 2 to 3 minutes. (Be careful not to overcook or the fish will become dry.) Remove from the pan and place on serving plates.

Using the same pan, sauté the shallot and zest. Pour in the wine and then the lemon juice. Add the capers and stir.

Finally add the parsley and pour the sauce over the sole filets.

Serve with boiled new potatoes.

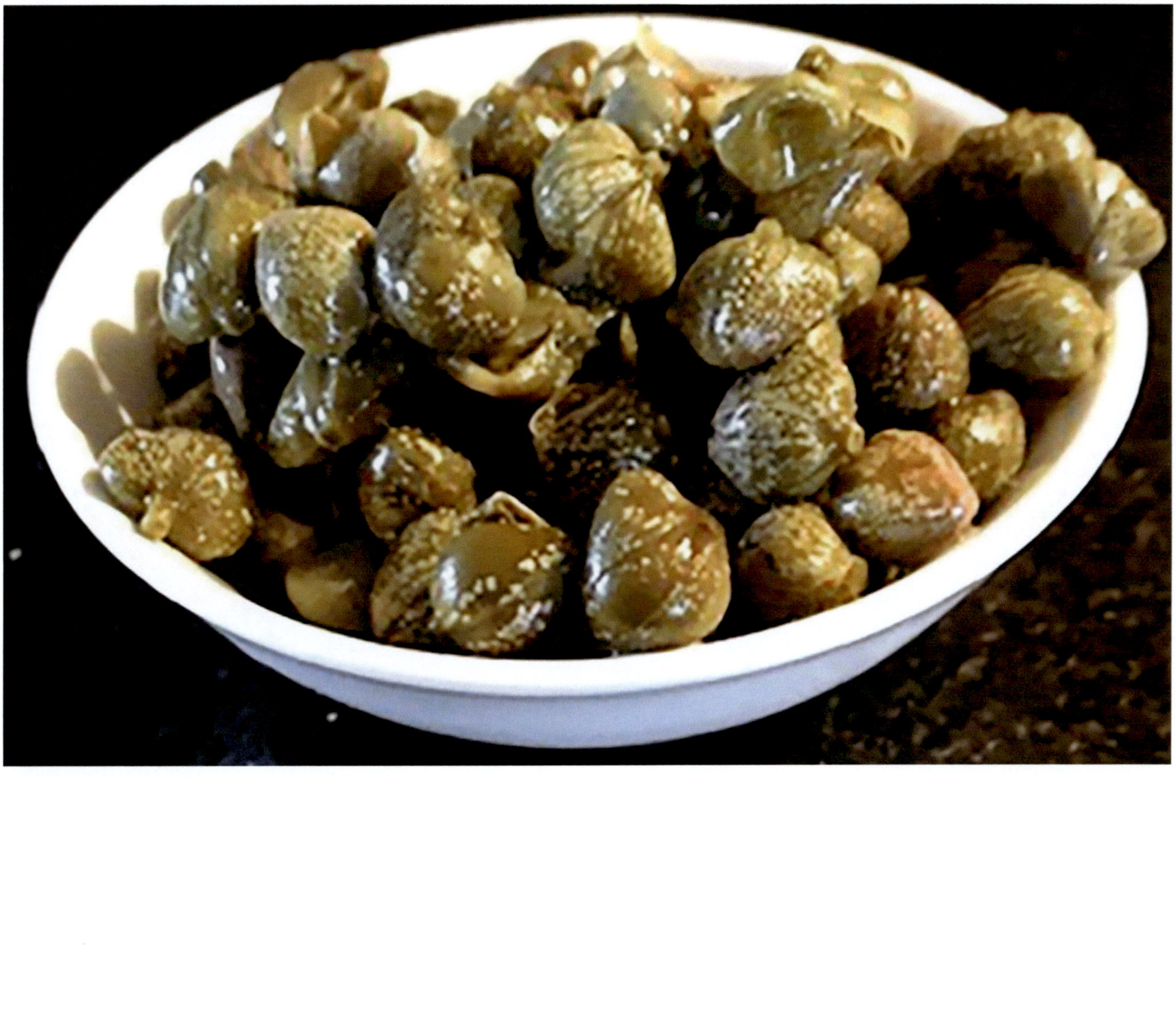

Cardamon

Recipe 12

Peach Crumble with Cardamom Crust

The far-eastern taste of cardamom transforms this Southern-American traditional favourite into an exotic dessert.

Dessert
Serves 4
Prep time: 30 minutes
Cooking time: 40 minutes

Ingredients

About 8 yellow peaches, halved, stones removed, and cut into wedges
2tbs caster sugar
Softened butter, for brushing
1tsp corn flour
2tbs coarse granulated sugar
Vanilla ice cream

Cardamom crust

300g/10 oz. plain flour
110g/4 oz. caster sugar
1tsp baking powder
1tbs ground cardamom
150g/half a cup cold unsalted butter in small pieces
150ml/5fl oz. milk

Method

For the cardamom crust

Sift flour, sugar, baking powder, cardamom, and ½ tsp salt into a bowl. Add butter and rub in with your fingertips until the mixture resembles fine crumbs. Add milk and combine by hand. Then gently knead until the mixture comes together.Serve with boiled new potatoes.

For the peach crumble

Preheat oven to 180°C/350°F. Butter a 9 inch (22 x 22 cm) ovenproof

59

baking dish. Combine peaches, sugar, and corn flour in a bowl and spoon into the baking dish. Using your fingers, crumble the cardamom dough over the peaches to cover, scatter with the sugar, and bake for 35 to 40 minutes or until golden and bubbling.

Serve hot with vanilla ice cream

Cardamon

Recipe 13

Boneless Tandoori Chicken

Main course
Serves 4
Prep time: 15 minutes
Marinating time: 4 to 8 hours
Cooking time: 30 minutes
Gluten-free

Ingredients

4 skinless chicken breasts
Vegetable oil

Marinade

4 cloves
1 tsp cumin seeds
1 tsp coriander seeds
4 green cardamoms, seeds only
2 black cardamoms, seeds only
1 tsp fenugreek seeds
1 tsp fennel seeds
250ml/1 cup full-fat plain yogurt
2 tbs fresh lemon juice
2 tsp salt
2 tbs sweet paprika
1 tsp ground turmeric
2 tbs fresh ginger, grated
2 tsp honey

Marinade

Heat a dry pan over medium heat. Add the cloves, cumin seeds, coriander seeds, cardamom seeds, fenugreek, and fennel. Toss the pan regularly to rotate the spices and prevent burning. Toast until they emit a very rich aroma: about 2 minutes. Immediately place the seeds in a dish to cool. Once cool, use a mortar and pestle to grind the spices to a powder.

Put the yogurt in a medium bowl and add the powdered spices along with the remaining marinade ingredients. Combine thoroughly.

Cut 2 or 3 shallow diagonal cuts into the top of each piece of chicken.

Place the chicken into a re-sealable plastic bag. Pour over the marinade, ensuring the chicken is thoroughly coated on all sides. Seal the bag and refrigerate for 4 hours, preferably more.

Preheat the oven to 250ºC/500ºF. Place a sheet of aluminium foil on a baking tray and place the chicken on top. Drizzle the vegetable oil over the chicken. (This prevents burning.)

Grill (or roast if your oven does not have a grill setting) for 30 minutes.

Serve immediately with rice or with naan bread.

Chili powder

Recipe 14

Gazpacho

A spicy cold soup for hot summer days

Starter
Serves 2
Prep time: 15 minutes
Chilling time: 30 minutes
Gluten-free

Ingredients

500g/1lb tomatoes
1 medium-sized cucumber, peeled, seeded, and quartered
1 shallot, finely chopped
Juice of 1 lime
1 tbs chili powder
2 tbs coriander powder
3 tbs olive oil
1 tsp fine sea salt
1 pinch sugar
1 tsp cumin powder

Method

Preheat oven to 180°C/350°F.

Place tomatoes in a shallow baking dish and add water until half the tomatoes are submerged. Bake for 30 to 40 minutes.

Remove tomatoes and cool. Then peel.

Make purée of the roasted tomatoes, cucumber, and shallots until they become a smooth liquid (about 5 minutes).

Add the spices, lime juice, and olive oil. Make its purée for another 3 minutes.

Chill for a minimum of 30 minutes, or ideally longer. Garnish with sprigs of coriander, wedges of lime, and chunky croutons (as you wish).

Chef's suggestion: add chilled steamed king prawns to create a more substantial first course.

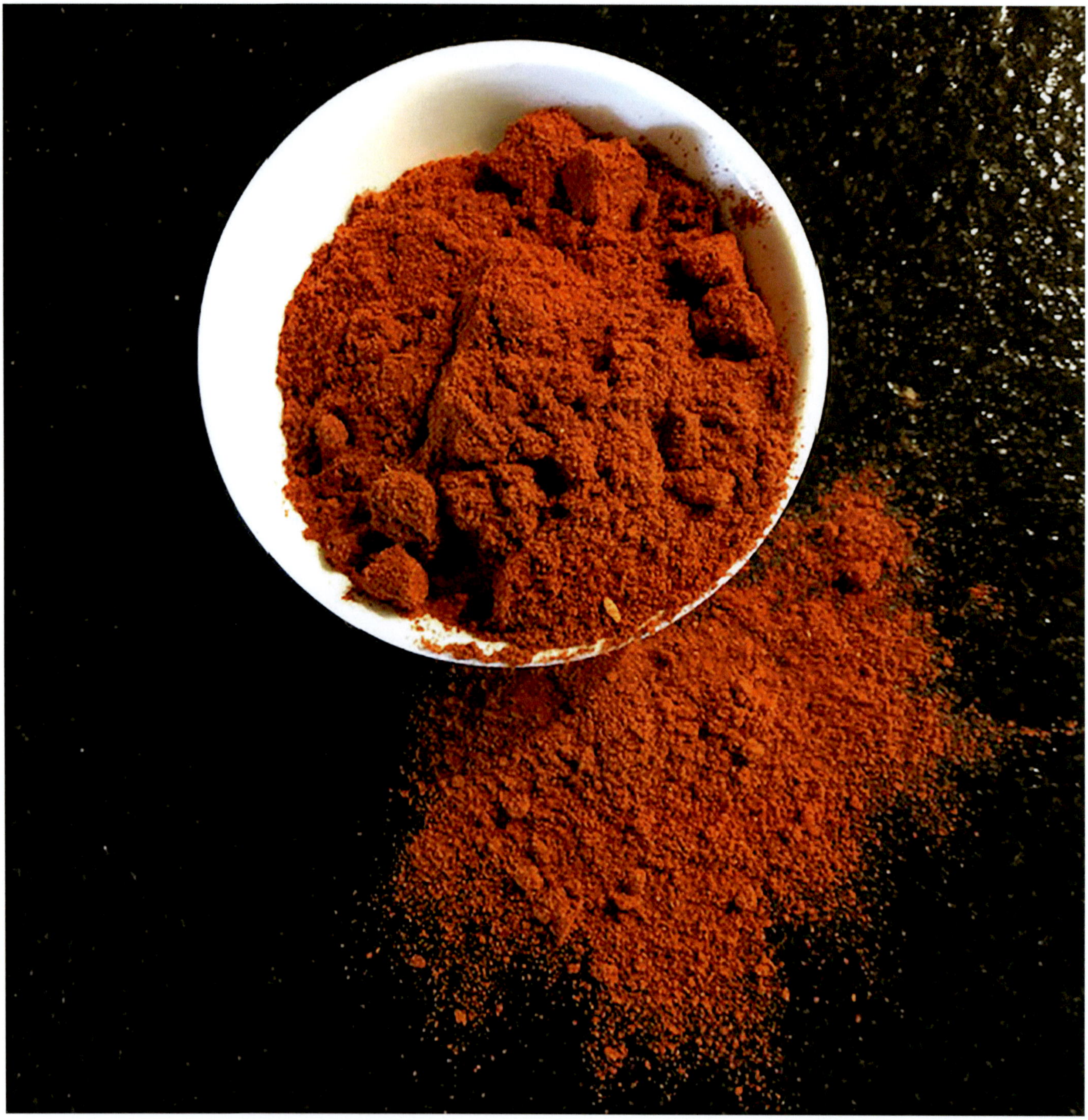

Chili powder

Recipe 15

Roasted Cauliflower with Chili

Great as a side dish with Sunday roast. Or dip into a cheese fondue for a gluten-free alternative to cubes of bread.

Side dish
Serves 4
Cooking time: 30 minutes
Gluten-free

Ingredients

1 large cauliflower, cut into florets
4 tbs olive oil
1 tbs chili powder
1 tsp sweet paprika
1 tsp ground cumin
1 tsp garam masala
Salt and pepper to taste

Method

Preheat oven to 200°C/400°F.

Wash and dry the cauliflower and place inside a re-sealable large plastic bag.

Add the chili powder, paprika, cumin, garam masala, and olive oil to the plastic bag.

Shake the contents so that the cauliflower is well coated and pour on to the baking tray.

Place into the oven and roast for 15 to 20 minutes.

Remove from oven and serve as desired.

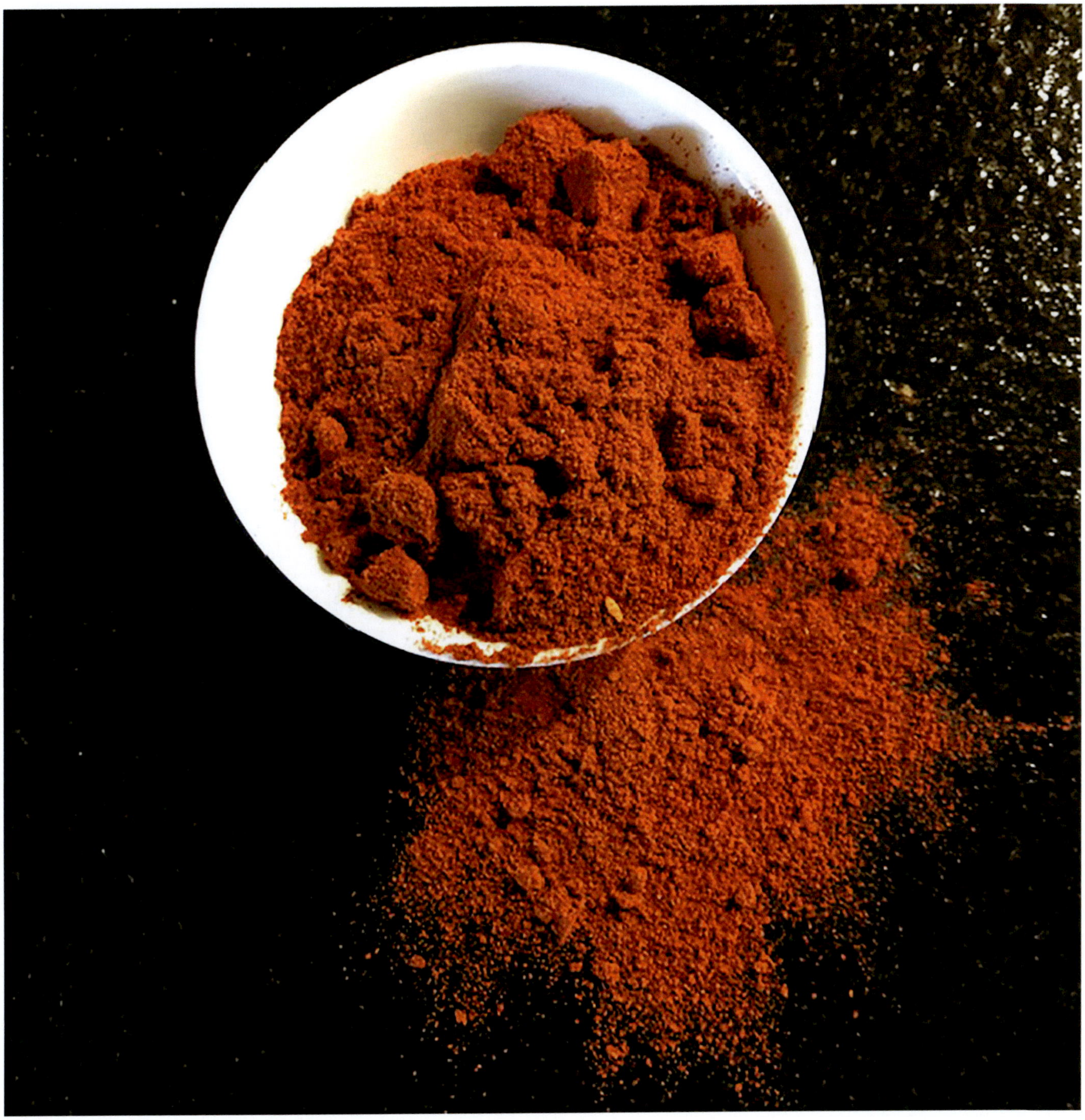

Chocolate

Recipe 16

Flourless chocolate cake

A cake where every bite bursts with rich, locked-in chocolate taste

Dessert
Serves 8 to 10
Prep time: 15 minutes
Cooking time: 45 minutes

Ingredients

500g/16 oz. chocolate, such as Lindt 64%
250g/1 cup unsalted butter
60ml/4fl oz. brewed espresso coffee
1tsp vanilla extract
8 large eggs
250g/1 cup sugar
Double-processed cocoa powder

Method

Preheat the oven to 220°C/425°F. Butter a deep spring-form pan 25cm square/10" square. Line the bottom and the sides with baking paper.

In a medium saucepan, melt the chocolate, butter, coffee, and vanilla over low heat until smooth.

In a bowl, using an electric mixer, beat the eggs and sugar until the mixture is thick and a pale-yellow colour (approximately 6 to 8 minutes).

Fold 1/3 of the egg mixture into the chocolate and mix for 2 minutes. Then add the rest of the mixture and beat for 5 minutes. Pour into the spring-form pan. Wrap the bottom and sides with aluminium foil to make pan watertight. Leave the top uncovered.

Create a bain-marie by placing the spring-form pan into a roasting dish with hot water reaching 2/3 up the sides of the spring-form pan. Bake for 5 minutes at 220°C/425°F. Then reduce to 180°C/350°F.

Butter a sheet of aluminium foil and now cover the top of the spring-form pan tightly and continue to bake for another 35 to 40 minutes.

Remove from bain-marie and dispose of foil. Let the cake cool in the spring-form pan for 2 hours. Then loosen the clip of the spring-form pan, peel off the baking paper, and flip the cake onto your serving dish. Dust double-processed powder cocoa over the top and serve with whipped cream and red berries.

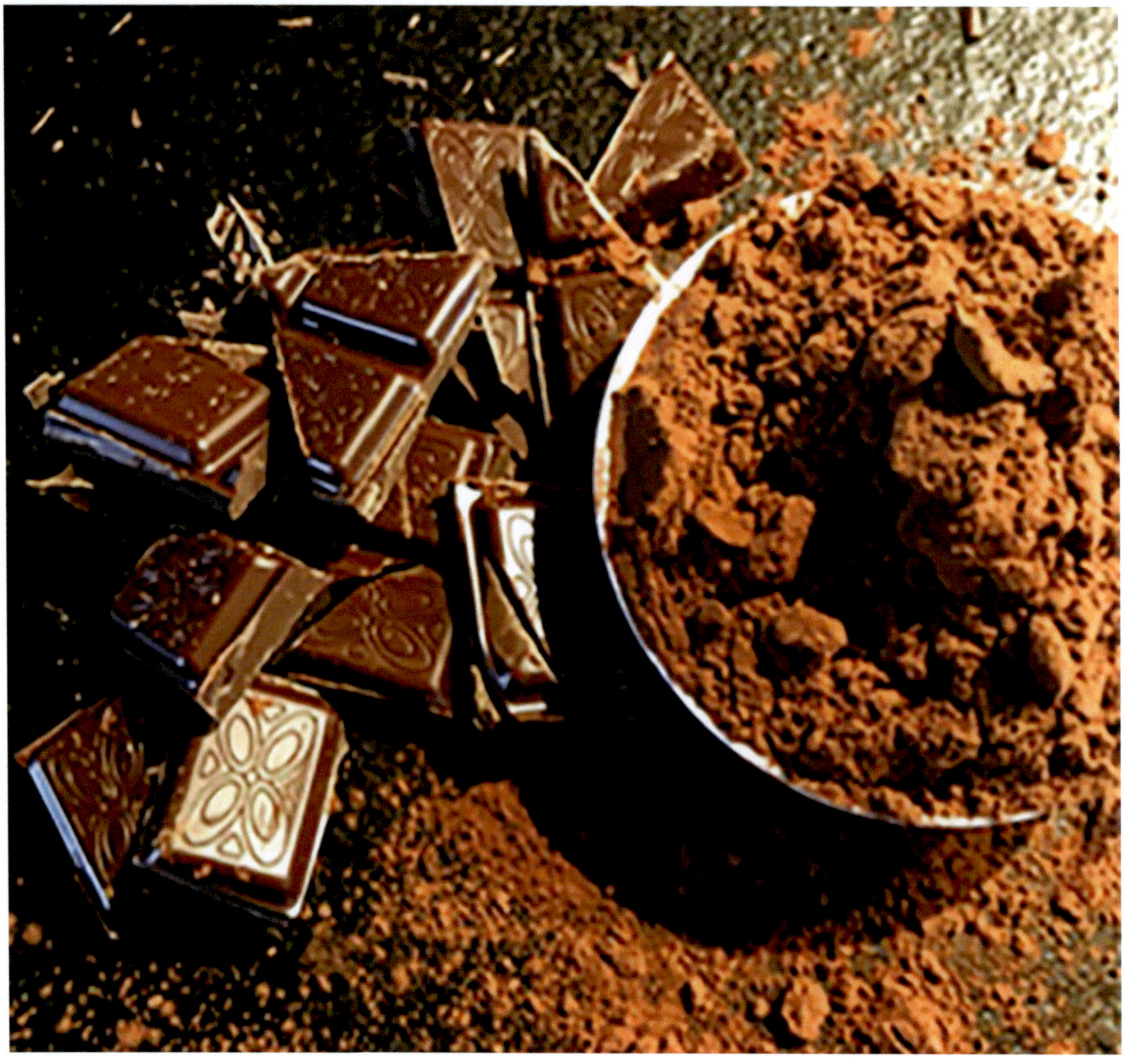

Cinnamon

Recipe 17

Forest-fruit Clafoutis

A version of this French classic, created to be gluten-free and dairy-free

Dessert
Serves 6
Prep time: 15 minutes
Cooking time: 45 minutes
Gluten-free
Dairy-free

Ingredients

500ml/1 cup fresh or frozen (and thawed) forest fruits, such blackberries and raspberries
5 to 6tbs caster sugar
1tbs dairy-free spread
85g/3 oz. gluten-free flour
1tbs ground cinnamon
4 eggs
400ml/13.5fl oz. coconut milk
Icing sugar, to dust

Method

Preheat oven to 180°C/350°F.
Drain the fruit. Toss berries with 1 tbs sugar. Then spread in an even layer in a 24cm/10" round ovenproof dish, greased with dairy-free spread.
Sift the flour and cinnamon into a large bowl and stir in the remaining sugar.
In another bowl, beat the eggs and coconut milk together. Then whisk into the flour mixture to make a smooth batter. Pour the batter slowly over the fruit. Then bake for 40 to 45 minutes.
Dust the clafoutis with icing sugar and serve.

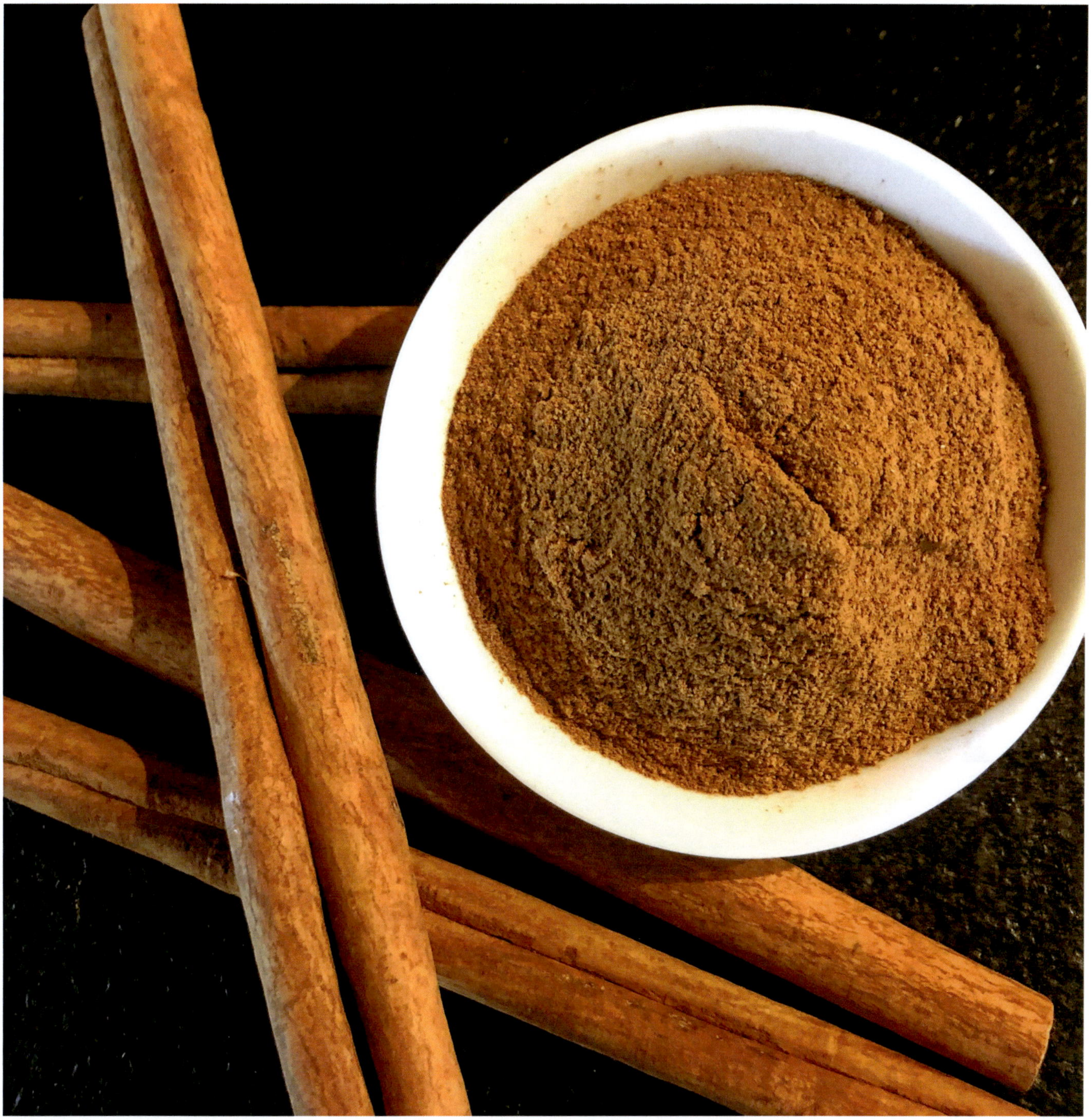

Cinnamon

Recipe 18

Luisa's banana bread

I designed this recipe during the 2008 financial crisis. I'm amazed, but perhaps not surprised, that it became a household staple again during Lockdown 2020.

Snack
Serves 6
Prep time: 20 minutes
Cooking time: 45 minutes

Ingredients

110g/4 oz. butter
250g/1 cup caster sugar
60ml/quarter cup honey
1tsp vanilla extract
2tbs cinnamon
2 eggs
75ml/3fl oz.
250g/1 cup mushy, very ripe bananas (about 3)
1tbs baking powder
Pinch of salt
250g/1 cup powdered almonds
500g/2 cups flour

Method

Preheat the oven to 180°C/350°F.
In a small saucepan, melt the butter and pour into a large mixing bowl. Add the sugar and mix using an electric standing or hand mixer until well blended. Then add the honey, vanilla extract, cinnamon, and eggs and continue to mix for 1 minute.
Add the bananas and mix until blended.
Add baking powder, salt, and powered almonds. Mix for 30 seconds.
Add half the flour, then the yogurt, and then the rest of the flour. Mix until blended. If your batter is too thin, add a little more flour.
Pour into a buttered and floured loaf pan and bake for approx. 45 minutes.
Test with a toothpick: if the toothpick comes out dry, then your banana bread is ready.

Loosen the bread from the sides of the loaf pan with a knife. Allow to cool completely before removing it from the loaf pan and slicing.

Cloves

Recipe 19

Roast Gammon with Mango Chutney Glaze

A traditional Boxing Day roast but delicious at any time of year

Main course
Serves 8
Prep time: 2 hours + 35 minutes
Gluten-free
Dairy-free

Ingredients

Gammon joint, rolled and tied, about 2.5kg/6lbs
1 large onion
2 carrots
6 cloves
2 bay leaves
2 sprigs of thyme
4 allspice berries
6 peppercorns

For the glaze

250g/1 cup mango chutney
120ml/half a cup cream sherry
24 Cloves for studding

Method

Put the gammon into a deep pan or casserole and cover with water. Boil for 5 minutes and then drain. Rinse away the white starch from the gammon and clean the pan.
Put the gammon back into the pan and cover again with water. Stud the onion with cloves and add it to the pan, along with the spices, herbs, carrots, and celery. Bring to the boil. Then reduce heat and simmer, covered, for 2 hours. Use a meat thermometer to check that the internal temperature has reached 63°C/145°F. Remove the gammon from the pan and place on a cutting board. Preheat the oven to 200°C/425°F.
Cut off the strings and outer crust of the gammon, exposing the fat on the top and leaving only a bit of the fat on the underneath side of the roast. Score a diamond pattern on the fat (the top side) and stud with the cloves.

For the glaze:
Put the mango chutney and the sherry into a small saucepan and boil until the liquid is nice and thick.

Brush the glaze over the gammon until it is well coated with the thick glaze. The glaze is a deep rich colour. Carve place the gammon back into the oven into slices and serve at 200ºC/400ºF and roast until (approx. 20 minutes)

81

Coffee

Recipe 20

Tiramisù

Inspired by the late Maida Heatter, it is definitely the best tiramisù recipe EVER! If serving as an evening dessert, why not use decaffeinated espresso coffee? Your guests will be grateful for your thoughtfulness.

Dessert
Serves 12
Prep time: 45 minutes
Chilling time: 4 to 12 hours
(But best if chilled overnight)

Ingredients

250ml/8fl oz. espresso, cooled
40 to 45 ladyfingers
450g/2 cups mascarpone
4 large eggs, separated
100g/half a cup granulated sugar
480ml/2 cups whipping cream
Pinch of salt
Unsweetened cocoa powder

Method

Use a large 20cm x 30cm/8" x 12" baking pan/dish with at least three-litre capacity. You will form 2 layers of dipped ladyfingers and mascarpone mousse.

First layer

Pour the espresso into a shallow bowl. One at a time, quickly dip each side of the ladyfingers. Do not oversaturate or make them soggy. Make a solid layer of the dipped ladyfingers in the baking pan. If necessary, cut some to fill empty spaces. Reserve remaining espresso and ladyfingers for the next layer.

For the mascarpone mousse

With a mixer, beat the mascarpone on medium speed in a large bowl until smooth. Set aside.

Put the egg yolks into a double boiler or use a heatproof bowl over a small pan of simmering water. Add 50g/quarter cup of the sugar and whisk for about 5 minutes until light and foamy. Remove from the heat and pour into the mascarpone. Beat on medium speed with a mixer until all is combined.

In a separate bowl, whip the heavy cream with a mixer until medium peaks form: about 3 to 4 minutes. Fold the whipped cream into the mascarpone mixture and set aside.

Add salt to the egg whites and beat at medium speed with a clean/dry whisk attachment for about 1 minute until foamy. Increase to high speed and slowly pour in the remaining 50g/quarter cup of sugar. Beat until stiff peaks form. It can take about 4 to 5 minutes. Gently fold the egg whites into the mascarpone mixture to make a mousse. Spread half of this mousse evenly over the bottom layer of ladyfingers.

Second layer

Dip remaining ladyfingers into the rest of the espresso and arrange one by one on top of the mascarpone mousse. Gently press each down so they are nice and compact.

Spread remaining mascarpone mousse evenly on top. If you're using a large enough pan/dish, it will fit but do not be afraid if it is puffy and higher than the sides.

Refrigerate uncovered for 2 to 3 hours. Then sift a dense layer of cocoa powder all over the top.

To serve

Using a sharp knife, slice the chilled tiramisù into servings. Wipe the knife clean between cuts. A small square metal spatula is very helpful to lift nice, clean squares out of the baking dish.

Cover any leftover tiramisu and store in the refrigerator for up to 3 days.

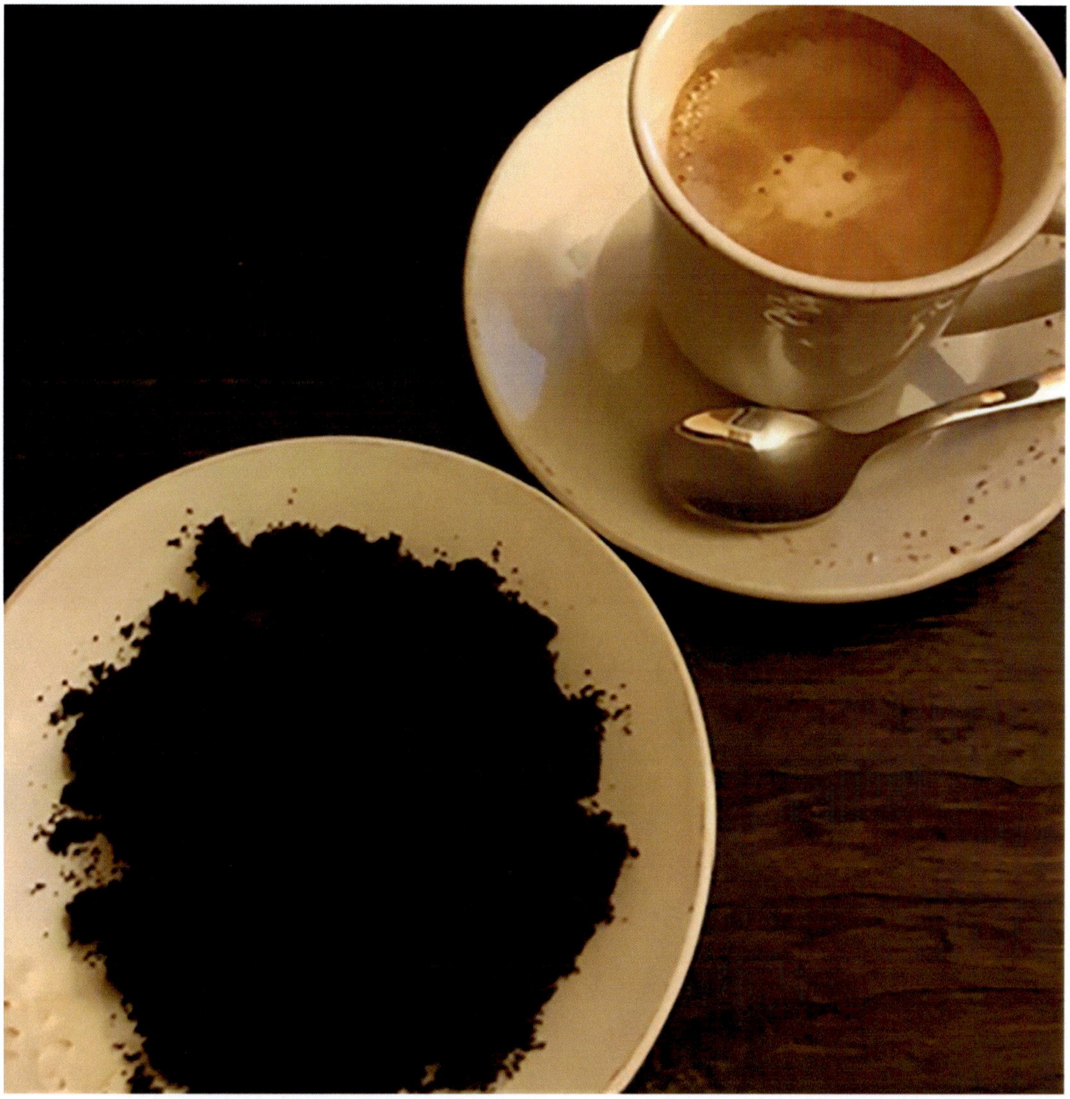

Coriander

Recipe 21

Gai Yang – Grilled Northeastern-Style Thai Chicken

The recipe was explained to me one evening by a Gai Yang vendor while I was shopping in the night market at Tha Sadet, Nong Khai, Thailand.

Main Course
4 Servings
Prep time: 15 min
Marinate time: 8 hours
Cooking Time: 35 minutes
Gluten-free

Ingredients

250ml/1 cup fish sauce or light soy sauce
3 green chili peppers, seeded and chopped
2 tbs sugar
3 shallots, finely chopped
200g/7 oz. fresh ginger, peeled and grated
Fresh lime juice from 4 limes
60ml/quarter cup water
1 large bunch fresh coriander (Preferably with roots)
1 large chicken, halved or cut up
Spring onions and coriander leaves for garnish

Method

With a mortar and pestle, pound the ginger. Then, one by one, add the coriander, shallots, and chilies and continue to pound. (Be careful not to get chili in your eyes while pounding – ouch!) Then stir in the lime juice, sugar, and water to complete the marinade. If the marinade is too salty, too sweet, or too hot, just add a little more water. (I'm not a fan of garlic, but for those who are, just add a few cloves at the pounding stage.)

Place the marinade into a large re-sealable plastic bag. Add the chicken and chill for 8 hours or up to a day.

Drain chicken and discard the marinade. Place the chicken on the BBQ or under the grill and cook thoroughly for approx. 35 minutes.

Transfer chicken to a platter. Garnish with spring onions and coriander leaves and serve with steamed sticky rice and individual bowls of dipping sauce, either a typical sweet chili sauce (Look for a Thai brand.) in an Asian specialty shop or try my recipe for 'versatile Thai dipping sauce' in this book.

Coriander

Recipe 22

Roast Pumpkin and Chickpea Salad with Coriander Dressing

This nutritious salad with exotic Indian flavours makes a satisfying lunch or supper.

Main course
Serves 2
Cooking time: 1 hour
Vegetarian
Gluten-free

Ingredients

500g/16 oz. pumpkin, seeded and cut into chunks
200g/7 oz. tinned chickpeas (Drained and rinsed)
2tsp ground cumin
2tsp ground coriander
2tsp smoked paprika
2tsp dried chili flakes
1 bag of fresh baby spinach
80g/3 oz. feta cheese, cubed
2tbs tahini
75ml/third of cup plain yogurt
1 lemon, juiced
1 bunch of coriander
4tbs extra virgin olive oil

Method

Preheat the oven to 200°C/400°F.

Coat the pumpkin with the olive oil and dried spices and toss until the pumpkin is well coated. Pour on to a baking tray and bake for 30 minutes. Add the chickpeas to the tray and bake for another 20 minutes.

While the pumpkin and chickpeas are baking, prepare the dressing by putting the yogurt, tahini, lemon juice, and fresh coriander into a mini food processor and whizz until the dressing is smooth and green.

Remove the baking tray from the oven (The vegetables should be well cooked and a bit charred and crispy.) and leave to cool for about 5 minutes. Pour the salad sauce on to the baked vegetables. Add the baby spinach and toss again.

Place on to individual serving plates. Crumble the feta over the top and serve.

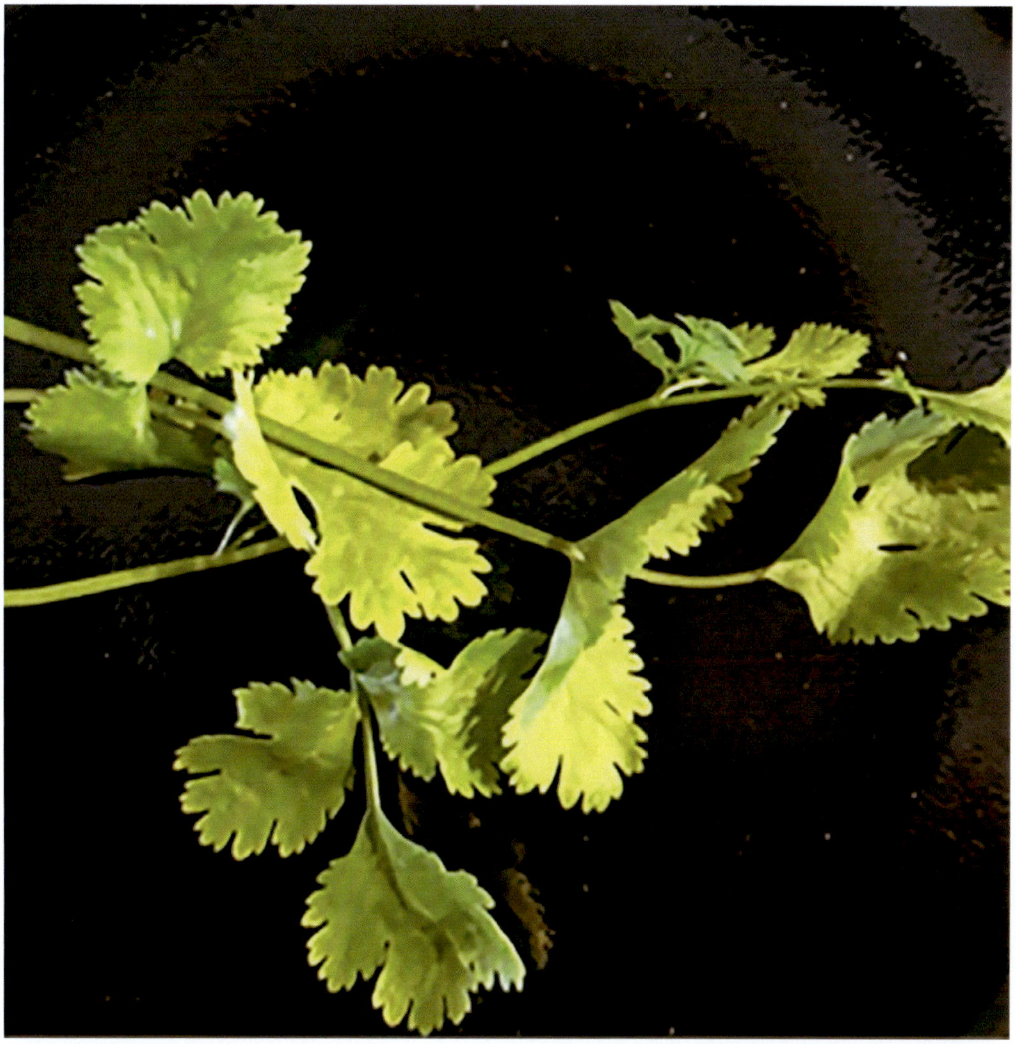

Cumin

Recipe 23

Moroccan-Style Couscous

A fabulous, nutritious side dish with easy-to-source ingredients: winter, spring, summer, and autumn

Side dish
Serves 4
Prep time: 10 minutes
Cooking time: 25 minutes
Dairy-free

Ingredients

1 large red bell pepper, cored, seeded, and sliced
2 medium carrots, cut in 2cm slices
1 small red onion, diced into chunks
2 small zucchini, halved lengthwise and cut into 2cm slices
4 tbs olive oil
2 tbs fresh lemon juice
2 tsp ground cumin
1 tsp ground coriander
1 tsp ground cinnamon
2 pinches of salt
400g/14 oz. dry couscous
450ml/2 cups chicken broth
2 tsp turmeric
175g/6 oz. dried apricots, sliced
80g/half cup slivered almonds
500g/2 cups chickpeas, drained and rinsed
1 tbs fresh coriander, minced
1 tbs fresh mint, minced
Slices chili peppers for garnish

Method

Preheat oven to 250°C/500°F. Place baking paper on to a baking tray. Add the pepper, carrots, onions, and zucchini. Drizzle with 1tbs of olive oil and season with salt. Toss to evenly coat. Roast in oven for about 20 minutes or until tender, tossing once halfway through roasting.

In a small mixing bowl, whisk together remaining 3tbs olive oil, lemon juice, cumin, coriander, and cinnamon while the vegetables are roasting. Season with a pinch of salt. Set aside.

In a saucepan, bring chicken broth, together with a pinch of salt and the turmeric, to a boil.

Now place couscous, apricots, and almonds in a large mixing bowl. Pour the hot chicken broth over the couscous and stir. Cover the bowl with plastic wrap and let rest for 10 minutes.

Add the roasted vegetables together with the chickpeas, coriander, mint, and lemon to the couscous and toss to evenly coat.

Taste and add more salt if desired. Garnish with chili peppers. Serve warm.

Cumin

Recipe 24

Tandoori Lamb Chops

A quick and easy method to enjoy a taste of India

Main course
Serves 4
Prep time: 10 minutes
Marinating time: 2 hours
Cooking time: 10 minutes
Gluten-free

Ingredients

8cm piece of ginger, grated
2 limes, zest and juice
1tbs coriander seeds
1tbs cumin seeds
1 pinch of garam masala
1 pinch of salt
1 large pinch dried chili flakes
8tbs pomegranate molasses
12 lamb chops, trimmed
A large bunch of mint leaves

Method

Toast the cumin and coriander seeds in a small frying pan for 30 seconds. Remove from heat and grind to a fine powder. Add the salt, garam masala and mix.

Add to this mixture the grated ginger, chili flakes, zest and lime juice, and 4 tbs of the pomegranate molasses. Pour into a large re-sealable plastic bag. Place the lamb chops into the bag and marinate for 2 hours. Turn the bag occasionally.

Heat your grill or grill pan to a high temperature and cook the lamb chops for 2 to 3 minutes on each side. The lamb chops will be slightly crispy and charred on the edges.

Place the chops on to a serving platter.

Drizzle the remaining 4 tbs of pomegranate molasses over the platter, sprinkle the pomegranate seeds, and toss liberally the torn mint leaves.

Serve with raita and roasted potatoes.

Curry powder

Recipe 25

Scallopini alla Milanese with Chicken

East meets west in this traditional Italian classic

Main course
Serves 4
Prep time: 15 minutes
Cooking time: 30 minutes

Ingredients

2 chicken breasts, sliced very thin, into 'scallopini'
250g/1 cup breadcrumbs
250g/1 cup flour
1tbs Madras curry powder
Pinch of salt
2 eggs
2tbs heavy cream
Juice of 1 lemon
100g/half cup parmigiano shavings
120ml/4fl oz. olive oil, plus some to drizzle
2tbs of butter
2 handfuls of arugula/roquette salad
3 tomatoes, quartered

Method

Mix the breadcrumbs and flour in a shallow bowl while adding the curry powder and salt.

In another shallow bowl, beat the eggs. Add the cream and continue until frothy.

Pour the olive oil into a large sauté pan. Add the butter and melt.

Dredge the scallopini of chicken into the egg mixture and then into the breadcrumb mixture. Then gently place into the hot oil.

Cook on one side for 7 minutes. Then flip and cook for an additional 5 minutes and drain on kitchen towels.

Using a large serving platter, make a bed of arugula/roquette salad, place your scallopini on top, and finish with a generous squeeze of lemon juice. Serve with quartered tomatoes and fresh parmigiano shavings.

Curry powder

Recipe 26

Curry Sauce for Ravioli

Ideal with salmon or crab ravioli, or almost any ravioli. Use prepared ravioli or make your own. The choice is yours.

Primo piatto
Serves 4
Prep time: 30 minutes
Cooking time for ravioli: 15 minutes

Ingredients
For the sauce

60ml/quarter cup olive oil
2 shallots chopped
2 leeks, white part only, washed and thinly sliced
1 fennel bulb, chopped
1 pear, peeled, cored, and thinly sliced
3tbs brandy
3tbs curry powder, a mild and very yellow one
2tbs corn flour
750ml/3 cups rich chicken stock
125ml/half cup coconut cream
Black sesame seeds and parsley for garnish

Method
For the sauce

Heat the olive oil in a large sauté pan over medium high heat. Add the shallots, leeks, and fennel and cook until they are soft in about 6 minutes. Reduce heat to medium. Add the pear and cook the mixture for 30 minutes, stirring occasionally.

Pour on the brandy. Allow it to heat and carefully ignite it using a long kitchen match. Swirl the pan until the flames die.

Add the chicken stock slowly, whisking constantly. Add the curry powder. Cook until the sauce begins to thicken. Then lower the heat and allow it to simmer uncovered for 20 minutes, stirring frequently.

Strain the sauce through a sieve into a medium saucepan.

Add the coconut cream to the sauce. Allow the sauce to simmer for 10 minutes.

For the ravioli

Prepare your favourite recipe or purchase fresh ravioli from the shop and follow the recommended cooking instructions.

Serve with fresh sprigs of parsley and toss black sesame seeds on top.

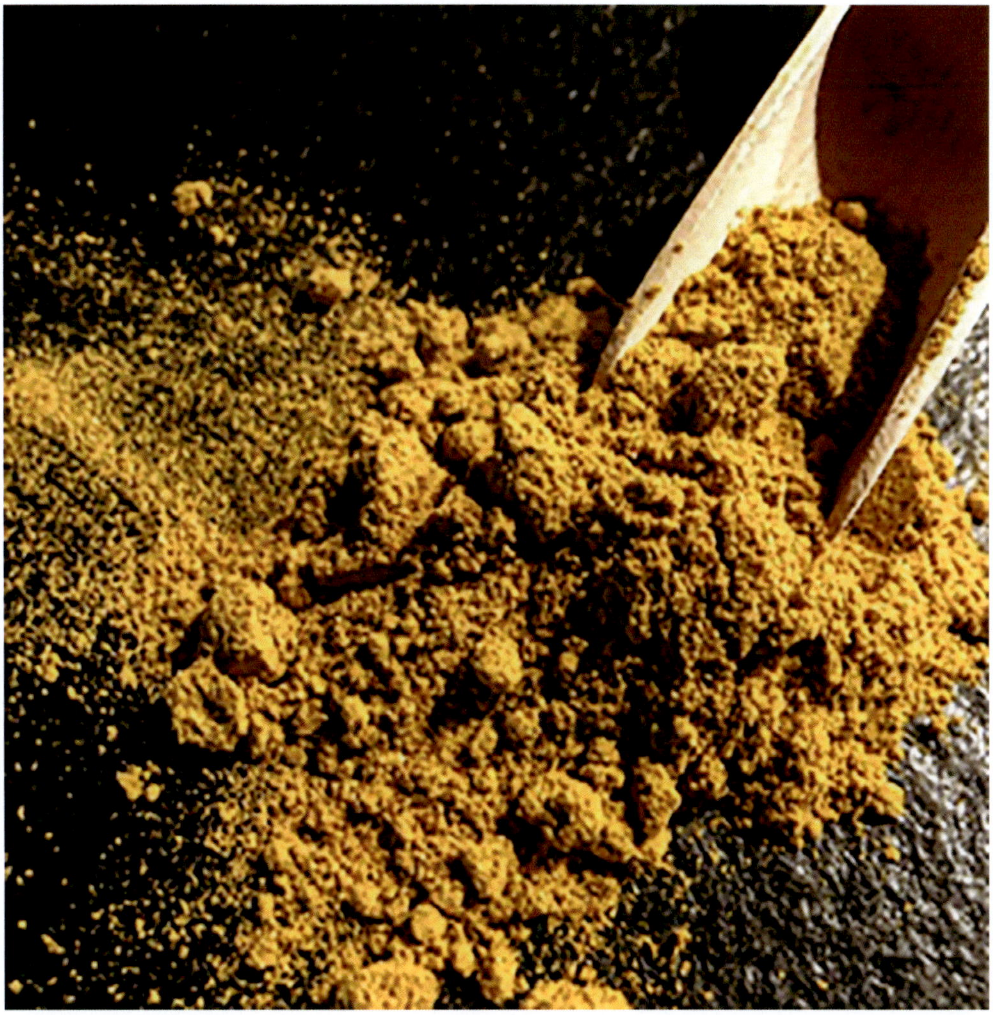

Dill

Recipe 27

Cucumber and Dill Salad

A quick and easy-to-whip-up summer-fresh favourite full of crisp tastes. A great complement to a BBQ

Side dish
Serves 4
Prep time: 10 minutes
Gluten-free

Ingredients

1 cucumber
250g/1 cup low-fat Greek-style yogurt
1 lemon, freshly squeezed
Bunch of fresh dill, fronds only
Salt and pepper to taste

Method

Peel and slice the cucumber and place into a mixing bowl.
Add the yogurt, lemon juice, and dill. Toss until well combined.
Add salt and pepper to taste.
Serve chilled.

Dill

Recipe 28

Gimme a gimlet, please!

Dill, such a sophisticated herb to sip!

Apéro
Serves 1
Prep time: 5 minutes

Ingredients

60ml/2fl oz. dry London gin
60ml/2fl oz. Rose's lime cordial
1 lime slice
Juice of half a lime
2 dill sprigs plus one to garnish
Ice cubes

Method

Fill half of the cocktail shaker with ice cubes.
Pour in the gin and lime cordial. Then squeeze in the lime and add 2 dill sprigs.
Place the lid on the shaker and shake until the sides become frosty.
Strain into a chilled martini glass.
Add the lime and the sprig of dill.
Serve!

Fenugreek

Recipe 29

Murgh Makhani (Indian Butter Chicken)

For years, I used to avoid Indian cuisine, until I tasted my friend Prisha's butter chicken! And now I am a convert.

Main course
Serves 4
Prep time: 20 minutes plus marination
Cooking time: 30 minutes

Ingredients

125ml/half a cup natural Greek-style yogurt
1tbs tandoori masala powder
500g/1lb boneless, skinless chicken breast, cut into 3cm pieces
1 onion, chopped
Large piece of fresh ginger
3tbs cooking oil
1tbs garam masala
1tspIndian chili powder
250ml/1 cup tomato passata
175ml/three-quarters cup coconut cream
2tbs butter
1tbs dried fenugreek leaves or 2tsp fenugreek powder
1tsp salt
For garnish: coriander leaves, lime wedges, and slivered almonds

Method

Stir the yogurt and tandoori masala powder together in a large bowl until combined. Add the chicken and toss to coat evenly. Marinate in refrigerator for 1 hour. Discard any excess marinade.

Purée the onion and ginger with a little water in a mini food processor until it forms a smooth paste. Set aside.

Heat 1tbs oil in a large frying pan over medium heat. Cook the chicken in the oil until lightly browned on all sides, for about 5 minutes. Remove from the frying pan and set aside. Heat the remaining 2tbs of oil in the pan. Fry the onion/ginger paste in for about 3 minutes. Add the garam masala and chili powder and cook for 1 minute more. Now pour in the tomato passata, reduce heat to medium-low, and cook for another 5 minutes. Return the chicken to the pan and add the coconut cream. Bring to a boil. Add the butter, fenugreek, and salt. Reduce heat to low and simmer uncovered until the chicken pieces are no longer pink in the middle, for 15 to 20 minutes.

Garnish with freshly torn coriander leaves, lime wedges, and almonds.

Serve with basmati rice and warm naan bread.

Galangal

Recipe 30

Tom Kha Goong (Thai Prawn and Coconut Milk Soup)

A perfectly balanced, elegant start to any celebration, whatever the type of cuisine. Not too spicy, not too tart, and not too sweet or salty

Starter
Serves 4
Prep time: 15 minutes
Cooking time: 10 minutes
Gluten-free
Dairy-free

Ingredients

200g/1 cup prawns, peeled
100g/4 oz. tofu, firm variety, cubed 500ml/2 cups chicken or vegetable broth
500ml/2 cups coconut milk
1tsp fish or soy sauce
1tbs shallots, minced
Juice of 2 limes
1 knob of galangal (if fresh cannot be found, use 50g/2 oz. galangal paste)
2 stalks of lemongrass, hard outer leaves removed, thinly sliced
4 white peppercorns
2tbs fresh ginger, minced
1tbs coriander leaves
2 red chili peppers, seeded and sliced
2 kaffir lime leaves, ripped so as to release their flavour

Method

Using a mortar and pestle, pound the white peppercorns into a powder. Then add the ginger and shallots. Continue to pound into a thick paste.

Pour the broth and coconut milk into a saucepan and heat to a boil. Add the galangal, ginger paste, fish sauce, lemongrass, and lime juice. Stir and boil for 10 minutes.

Add the prawns and tofu. Cook for 3 minutes and stir gently so that the tofu stays in its cubed form.

Remove the knob of galangal.

To serve: pour the soup into a large bowl and top with the coriander leaves,

sliced chilies, and the kaffir lime leaves.
   Or serve with a portion of steamed jasmine rice as a small meal in itself!
   Variation: chicken breast sliced in chunks can be an alternative to prawns. Adjust the cooking time to 15 minutes.

Galangal

Recipe 31

Gaeng Keow Waan Gai (Thai Green Curry with Chicken)

It is my husband's favourite. If left to his own devices, he would eat this every day! I hope that you find this authentic recipe equally additive.

Main course
Serves 4
Prep time: 40 minutes
Cooking time: 35 minutes
Gluten-free
Dairy-free

Ingredients

5 green Thai chili peppers, seeded and chopped
4tbs fresh ginger, minced; or 5tbs ginger paste
2 shallots, minced
1 bunch of fresh coriander (with roots is best if you can find)
2 stalks of lemongrass, sliced
Juice of 2 limes
2tbs fish sauce
5 white peppercorns
2tbs sugar
2 pinches of salt
250ml/1 cup of chicken broth
400ml/14fl oz. coconut milk
250ml/1 cup coconut cream
A 4cm piece of galangal or 2tbs of galangal paste
2 chicken breasts, sliced into bite-sized pieces
5 kaffir lime leaves (three for the curry and two to garnish)
3 Thai green eggplants (from Asian markets, or use courgettes).
Bunch of Thai pea eggplants (omit if you can't find.)
2 tomatoes, quartered
1 large potato, in chunks

Method

First, make the green curry paste either in a food processor, or for a richer flavour, use the ancient method of adding ingredients one at a time to a mortar and pestle. First, pound the white peppercorns into a powder. Then add, one after the other, green chilies, ginger, shallots, coriander, lemongrass, lime juice, fish sauce, sugar, and salt, then pounding after each to make a thick green paste. Trust me; this is not as complicated as it sounds! Alternatively, simply pulse all the above ingredients in a food processor.

In a large saucepan, bring the chicken broth and coconut milk to a boil. Add the galangal and the potato (not authentic, but the starch thickens and adds texture). Now add your green curry paste and stir.

Next add all the eggplants, tomatoes, and 3 torn kaffir lime leaves. Continue stirring.

Then add the chicken and coconut cream. Stir and reduce heat to a simmer and cook for 30 minutes. Remove the galangal and the dark green kaffir lime leaves.

Spoon the curry into a serving bowl and garnish with freshly torn kaffir lime leaves and serve with steamed jasmine rice.

Variant: Replace the chicken with prawns or tofu.

Garam masala

Recipe 32

Chicken Tikka

Pssssssst! A chef's secret… For the most tender grilled chicken, marinate in Indian tonic or green papaya paste for 4 hours. You'll be so happy that you did!

Serves 4
Prep time: 30 minutes plus marination
Grilling time: 12 minutes
Gluten-free

Ingredients

2 whole boneless chicken breasts
120ml/half cup of Indian tonic or green papaya paste (store bought in fine)
150g/5 oz. natural full-fat Greek-style yogurt
100g/4 oz. ginger paste
1tsp ground cumin
1tsp ground coriander
1tsp red chilli powder, plus extra if required
1tsp turmeric
2 limes, juice only
2tsp garam masala powder
Salt and white pepper, to taste

Method

   Cut the chicken breast into large cubes and place into a re-sealable plastic bag. Add the Indian tonic or the green papaya paste into the bag. Seal and put into the refrigerator for marinate for 4 hours.
   In a bowl, add the yogurt and all the remaining ingredients. Blend to a smooth paste. Taste and add more chili powder if needed.
   Drain the chicken and mix into the yogurt mixture. Cover with cling film and leave the chicken to marinate for 4 to 5 hours.
   Prepare and light the BBQ.
   Skewer the chicken pieces and place on to the hot grill. Cook for 10 to 12 minutes, turning occasionally.
   Serve with mango chutney and rice.

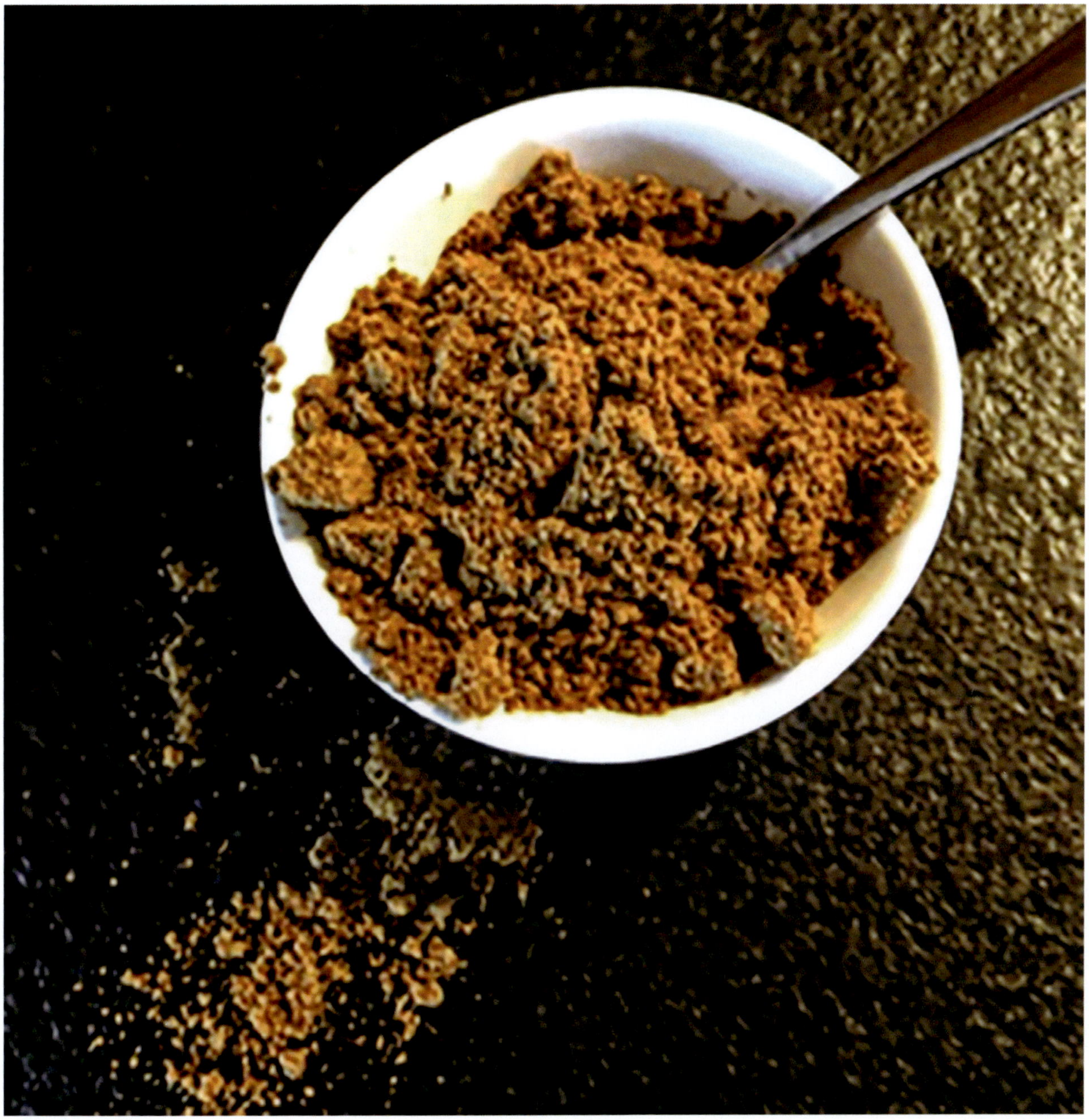

Garam masala

Recipe 33

Poached Peaches with Ricotta Buttercream and Crunchy Panko Topping

A savoury and refreshing summer salad with just a touch of sweetness

First course
Serves 4
Prep time: 10 minutes
Cooking time: 10 minutes

Ingredients

3 ripe large yellow peaches, thinly sliced
200g/7 oz. sugar
Juice of 1/2 lemon
3 cloves
200g/7 oz. fresh ricotta cheese
3tbs of natural Greek yogurt
2tbs unsalted butter
A bed of arugula/roquette salad
Honey drizzle
Panko breadcrumbs, toasted
1tbs garam masala

Method

Dissolve the sugar in 250ml/1 cup of boiling water. Add the sliced peaches, lemon juice, and cloves and poach for 10 minutes. Let the peaches cool in the liquid.

In a mini food processor, blend the ricotta cheese, butter, and yogurt until smooth.

Make a bed of the salad on a serving platter. Layer the poached peaches and dollop the ricotta mixture on top. (Reserve the liquid for another use: delicious when added to a Bellini cocktail or to make peach confiture.)

Finally, drizzle the finest honey that you have and sprinkle the toasted panko breadcrumbs and garam masala.

Serve with Parma ham and freshly baked focaccia.

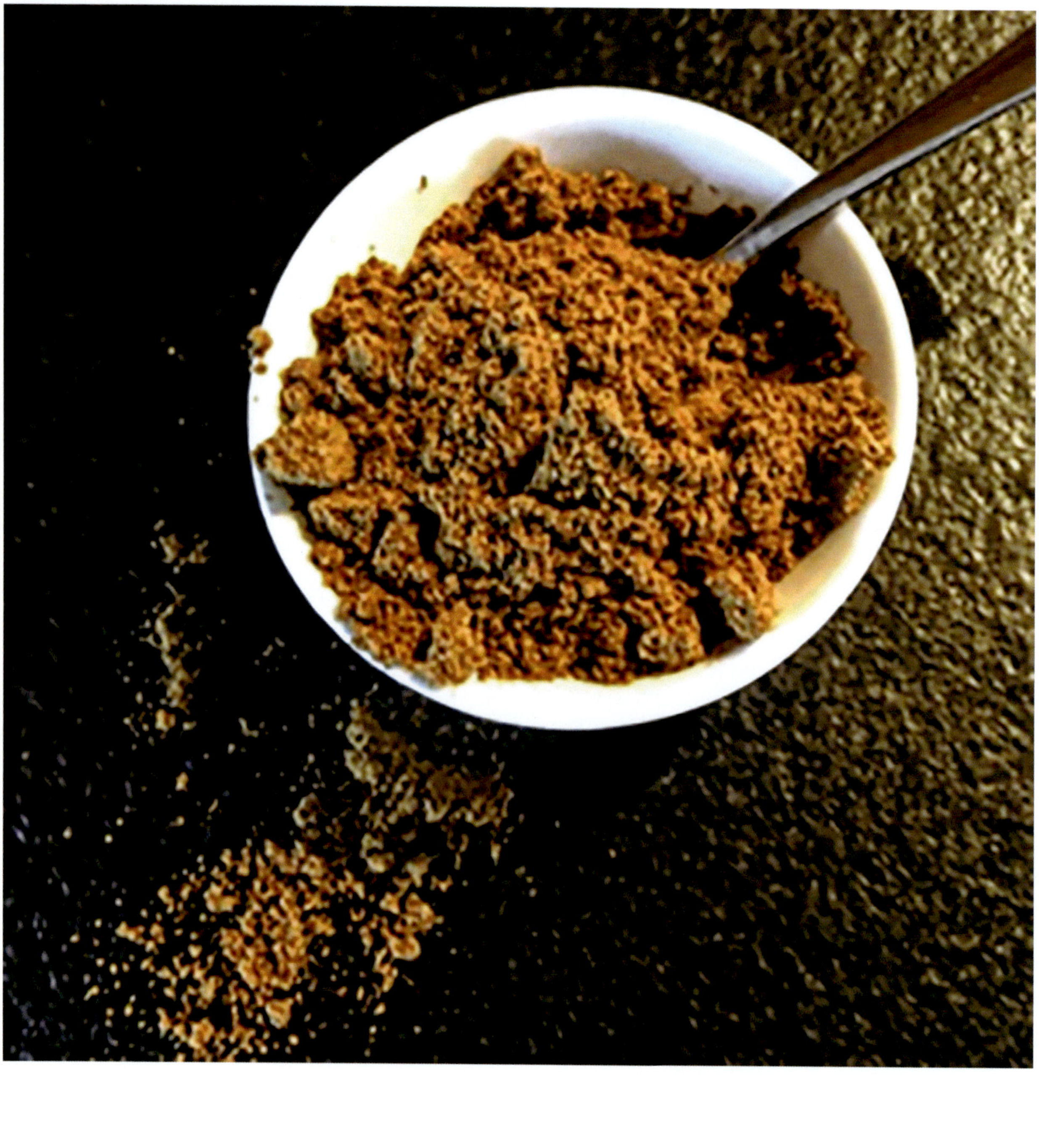

Ginger

Recipe 34

Thai Moo Sarong (Pork Wrapped in Golden Threads)

A recipe from the Ayutthaya Era (1351 – 1767) when Chao Wang food was created and chefs prepared specialties for the royal family and the court. A bit fiddly but worth the learning curve. Give it a try?

Starter
Serves 4
Prep time: 30 minutes plus chilling time
Cooking time: 5 minutes

Ingredients

250g/8 oz. minced pork
1tsp fish or soy sauce
1tbs shallots, minced
Juice of 1/2 lime
1tbs coriander stems and root, minced (or use coriander leaves if root unavailable)
2tbs fresh ginger, minced
8 whole white peppercorns
5 salt flakes
1tsp sugar
1 egg yolk
2tbs corn flour
100g/4 oz. of thin Asian egg noodles (use tagliolini if these are difficult to find)
250ml/1 cup vegetable oil for deep frying

Method

Using a mortar and pestle, pound the white peppercorns into a powder. Add the salt flakes, then the coriander root, ginger, and shallots. Continue to pound into a thick paste.

In a separate bowl, combine the egg yolk with the minced pork. Then add the corn flour, fish sauce, lime juice, and ginger/coriander paste and mix thoroughly.

Place the pork mixture into the refrigerator for 15 minutes to allow the flavours to blend. (It will become sticky; that's good.)

Remove from refrigerator and, by rolling between your fingers, create small balls. Chill for 20 minutes.

While the pork balls are chilling, cook the egg noodles in salted boiling water (with a drop of oil in the water) for approx. 3 minutes. Drain and pour cold water over the noodles. Drain again and separate the noodles with your fingers and lay flat on a lined tray

Wrap each meatball with 5 cooked noodles, one at a time, as if you are making a ball of string. Tuck in the end of each noodle to prevent unravelling.

Heat the vegetable or soy bean oil in a deep saucepan and fry each ball until it becomes golden and crispy. Drain on kitchen towels.

Serve with Thai sweet chili sauce, fresh slices of cucumber, and coriander leaves. Do not skimp on the presentation – you are creating food fit for kings and queens!

Variation: try minced prawns or chicken as an alternative to the porkdelicious when added to a Bellini cocktail or to make peach confiture.)

Finally, drizzle the finest honey that you have and sprinkle the toasted panko breadcrumbs and garam masala.

Serve with Parma ham and freshly baked focaccia.

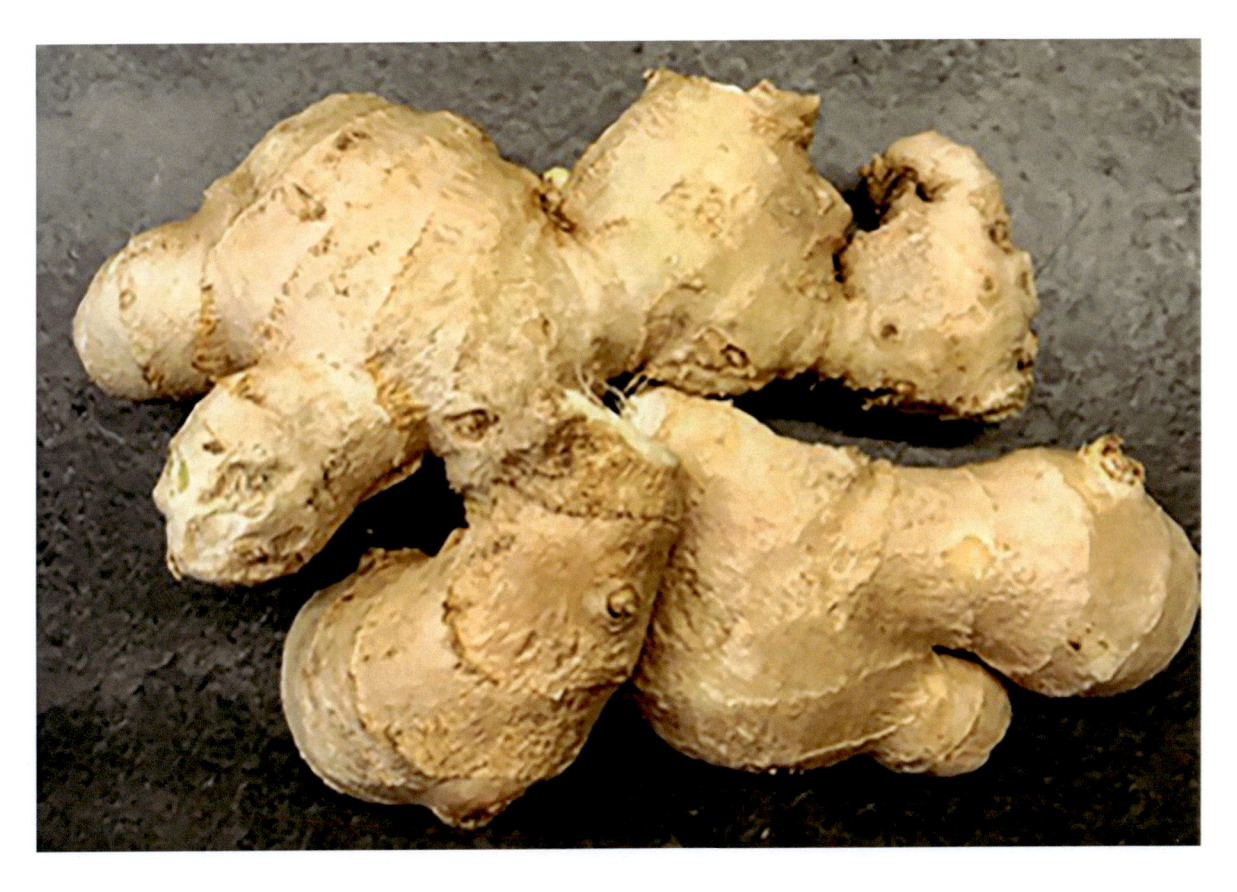

Ginger

Recipe 35

Thai Sweet Chili Sauce

A spicy sauce designed for dipping!

Sauce
Serves 4
Prep time: 5 minutes
Cooking time: 5 minutes

Ingredients

120ml/1cup rice vinegar
50g/quarter cup sugar
2tbs fresh ginger, minced
2tsp hot chili peppers, chopped
1tsp ketchup
Pinch of salt
1tsp corn flour

Method

Pour the vinegar and 50ml/quarter cup of water into a small saucepan and bring to a rapid boil.

Stir in the sugar, ginger, chili peppers, and ketchup. Simmer for 5 minutes.

In a mug, dissolve the corn flour in a little hot water. Stir vigorously to remove any lumps and whisk into the sauce until it thickens.

Pour into a serving bowl. Cover and allow to cool.

Dip your favourite Asian appetisers into the sauce and enjoy!

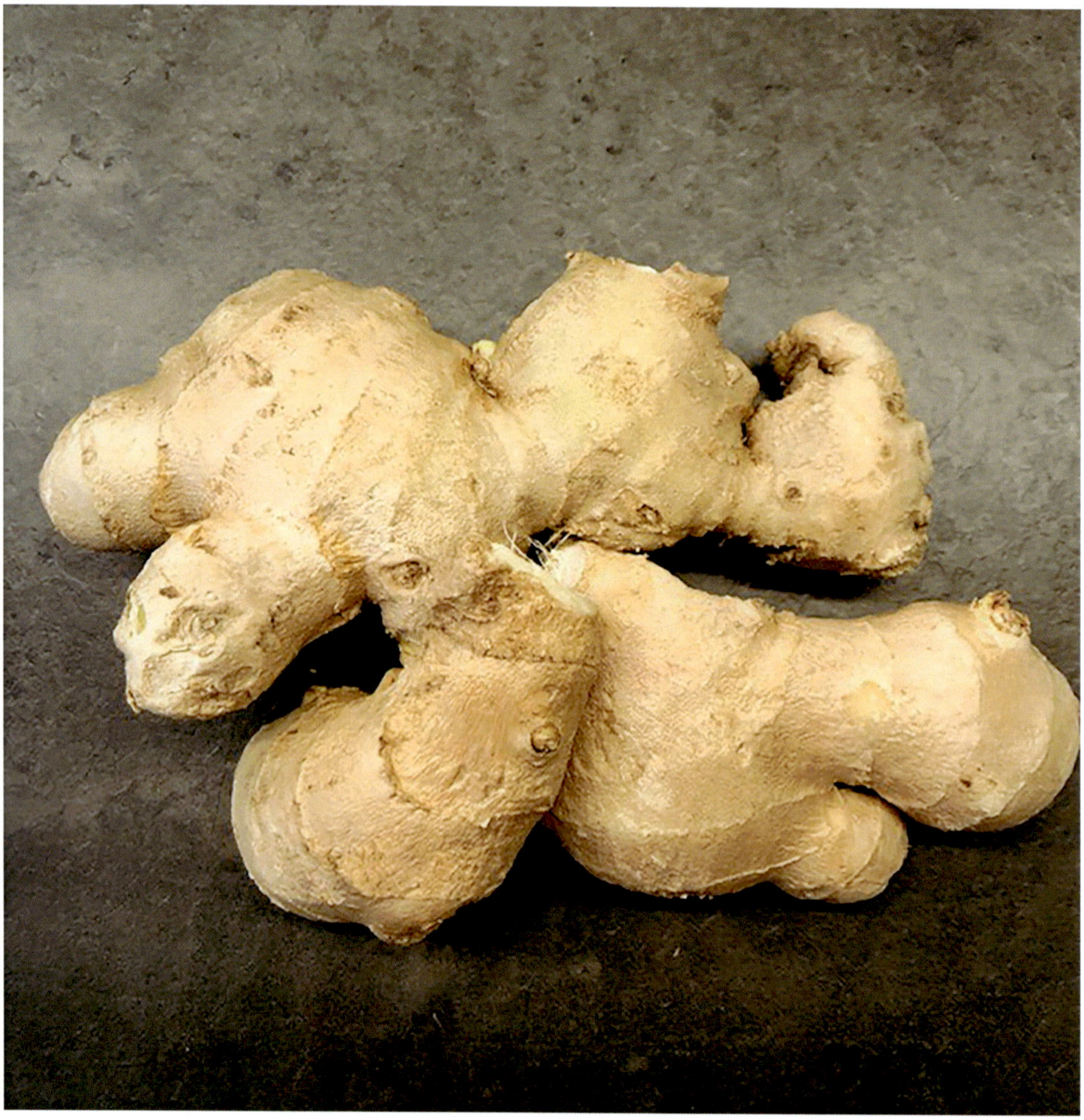

Ginger

Recipe 36

Versatile Spicy Thai Savoury Sauce

A salty, spicy, and savoury sauce. So versatile: as a salad sauce, a marinade for grilled meats and vegetables, or as a dip for spring rolls or dumplings.

Sauce
One portion
Prep time: 10 minutes

Also see video on my YouTube channel: lockedintastes

Ingredients

60ml/quarter cup fish sauce, soy sauce or teriyaki sauce
60ml/quarter cup freshly squeezed lime juice
30ml/1fl oz. water
2 red chilies, seeded and cut with scissors
125g/half cup of finely grated ginger
2 pinches of sugar

Method

Pour the liquid ingredients into a glass jar and shake. Then add the ginger, sugar, water, and chili and shake again.
The sauce can be stored for up to a week in the refrigerator.

Suggestion

If using the sauce as a marinade, also add a drizzle of sesame oil.

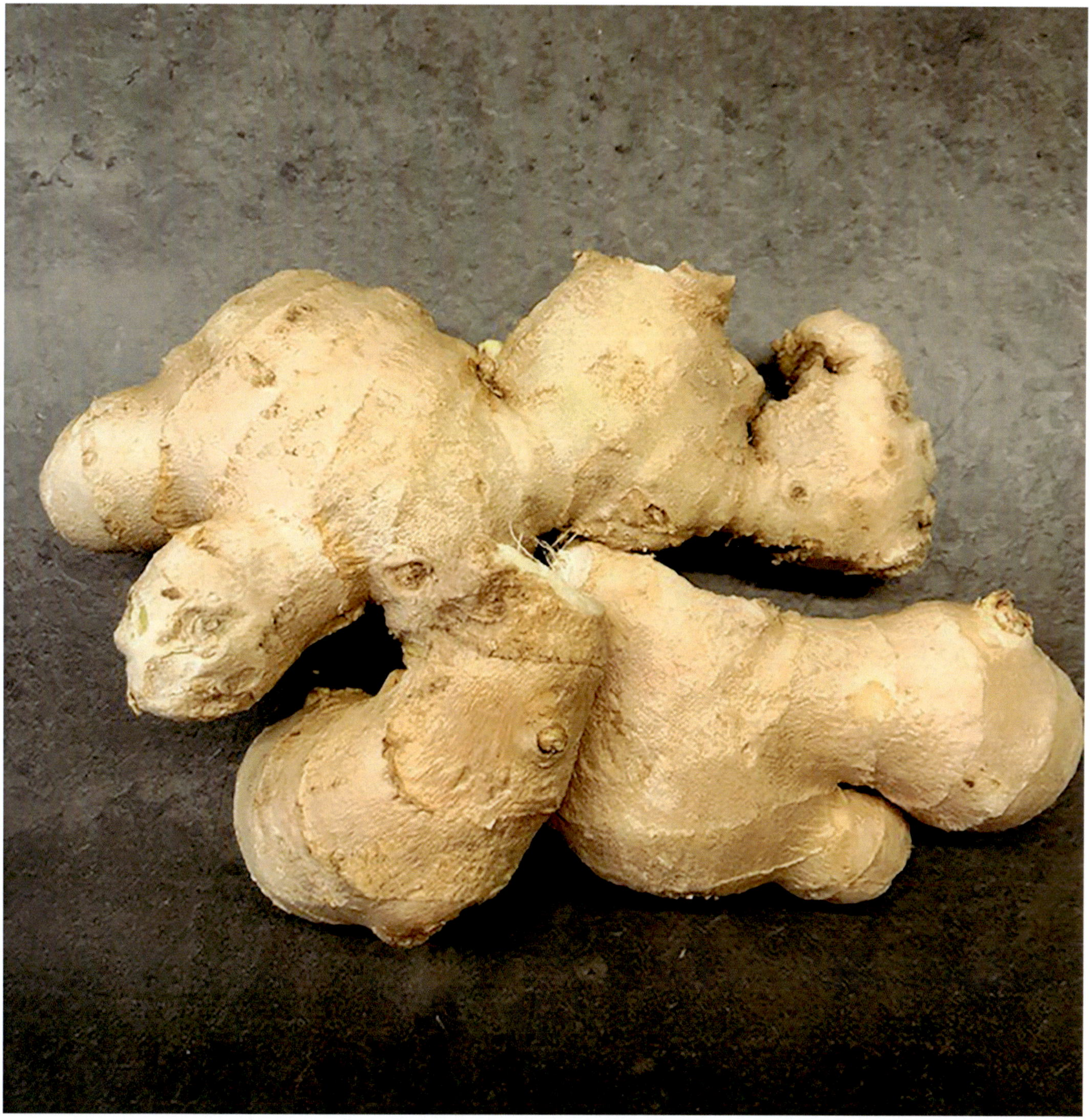

Grenadine

Recipe 37

A Swiss Kiss

A cocktail not to miss!

Apéro
Serves 2
Gluten-free
Vegetarian, vegan

Also see video on my YouTube channel: lockedintastes

Ingredients

One part dry gin
One part grenadine
One part fizzy lemonade
One freshly squeezed lemon

Method

Fill a cocktail shaker with ice cubes.
Pour the gin, grenadine, and lemon juice into the shaker.
Shake until the sides of the cocktail shaker become frosty.
Pour into martini glasses.
Top with the fizzy lemonade.
Serve.

Grenadine

Recipe 38

Singapore Sling

Inspired by Raffles Hotel, Singapore

Apéro
Serves 1

Ingredients

1tsp Cointreau
120ml/4fl oz. pineapple juice
15ml/1tbs lime juice
60ml/2fl oz. gin
2tsp grenadine
1tsp cherry liqueur
A dash of angostura bitters
1tsp DOM Benedictine
A splash of soda water to give the cocktail a bit of fizz. Or try tonic water instead

Method

Fill a cocktail shaker with ice. Pour all ingredients (except for the soda/tonic water and cherry liqueur) into the shaker. Shake until the outside of the shaker becomes nice and frosty.

Strain into highball glasses filled with ice cubes and top up with the soda or tonic water.

Drizzle the cherry liqueur on top and garnish with a slice of lime… and sip!

Herbs of Provence

Recipe 39

Roast Whole Chicken

There are many ways to cook a chicken, but this is the typical French bistro way. Why not try it at home?

Main course
Serves 4
Prep time: 10 minutes
Cooking time: 45 minutes
Gluten-free

Ingredients

1 whole chicken, rinsed
2 lemons, sliced in half
2tbs Herbs of Provence
60ml/quarter cup olive oil
60g/quarter cup unsalted butter, cut into chunks
Salt and pepper to taste
120ml/half cup brand or cream sherry
120ml/half cup chicken bouillon

Method

Preheat oven 200°C/400°F.

Place the chicken in a roasting pan with the breast side facing up. Rub the surface of the chicken with olive oil on all sides.

Squeeze the lemons on to the chicken. Then place the squeezed lemons into the cavity.

Sprinkle the Herbs of Provence on top of the chicken and season with salt and pepper.

Press the butter firmly on the breast so that it does not slide off.

Pour the chicken bouillon and brandy/cream sherry over the chicken, allowing the excess to collect in the roasting pan.

Roast for 45 minutes. You will know that the chicken is cooked when clear juices run from the meat and the skin is golden-brown and crispy.

Remove from oven and leave to rest for 10 minutes.

Remove the lemons from the cavity. Carve and serve with pommes frites.

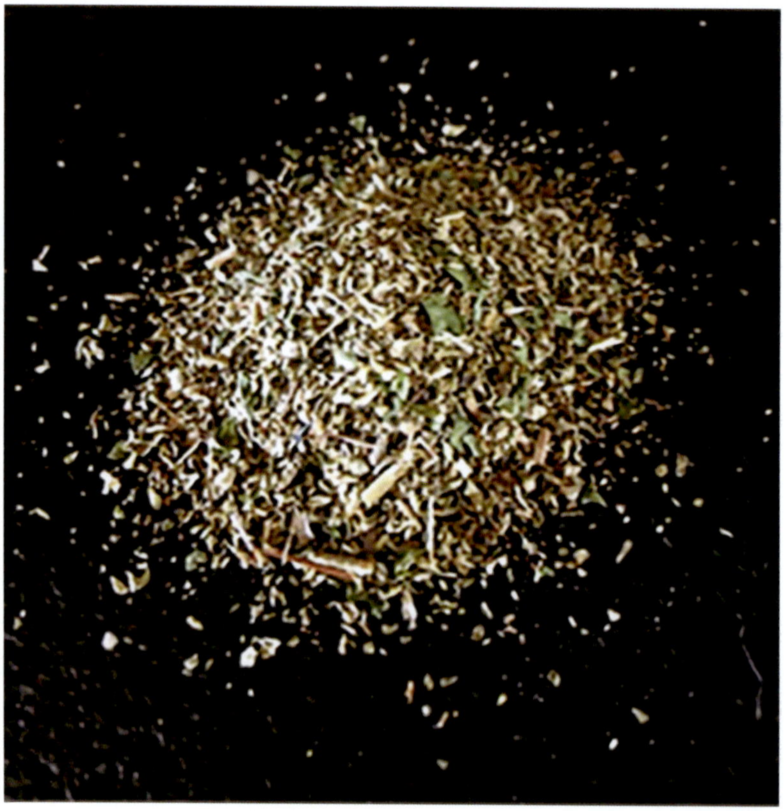

Juniper berries

Recipe 40

The Remedy – G and T

The imperial cocktail and tonic that kept the British healthy while battling malaria across the Empire. So it's not just a drink but a remedy!

Apéro
Serves 1
Mixing time: 5 minutes

Ingredients

60ml/quarter cup gin
150ml/5fl oz. Indian tonic
1/2 lemon

Method

In highball glass with ice, squeeze the lemon.
Pour the gin and then top up with the tonic.
Swirl with a non-metallic stirrer and serve.

Kaffir lime leaves

Recipe 41

Yam Wun Sen – Seafood and Cellophane Noodle Salad

This Thai noodle salad is a perfect crispy, spicy seafood starter to any meal. My version uses the cool flavours of lime leaves to calm the hot chili zing.

Starter
Serves 6
Cooking time: 10 minutes
Dairy-free

Ingredients

200g/7 oz. Wun Sen noodles: thin, threadlike 'cellophane' noodles
400g/14 oz. baby scallops, rinsed
300g/10 oz. prawns, peeled and deveined
1 tablespoon vegetable oil
2 shallots, peeled, finely sliced
2 plum tomatoes, cut into wedges
125g/half cup fresh coriander leaves
2tbs toasted peanuts, chopped
6 kaffir lime leaves, torn
2 red chili peppers, seeded and sliced
Dressing: versatile spicy Thai
savoury sauce, (recipe included in this book)

Method

Soak the noodles in lukewarm water in a bowl for 10 minutes to soften slightly. Drain.

Bring a large saucepan of water to the boil. Cook the noodles for 1 minute. Drain and transfer the noodles back to the bowl. Use scissors to cut them into 10cm/4" lengths.

Place the baby scallops and prawns in another bowl. Add the oil and toss to combine. Then stir fry in a wok at high heat to cook for 2 or 3 minutes.

Remove the scallops and prawns from the wok and transfer them to the bowl of noodles, tossing them together and adding the dressing (the versatile Thai savoury sauce) and also the shallots, tomato, coriander, and chili peppers. Transfer to a serving plate. Sprinkle with the peanuts and the torn kaffir lime leaves and chilies.

Serve with cucumber slices and lime wedges.

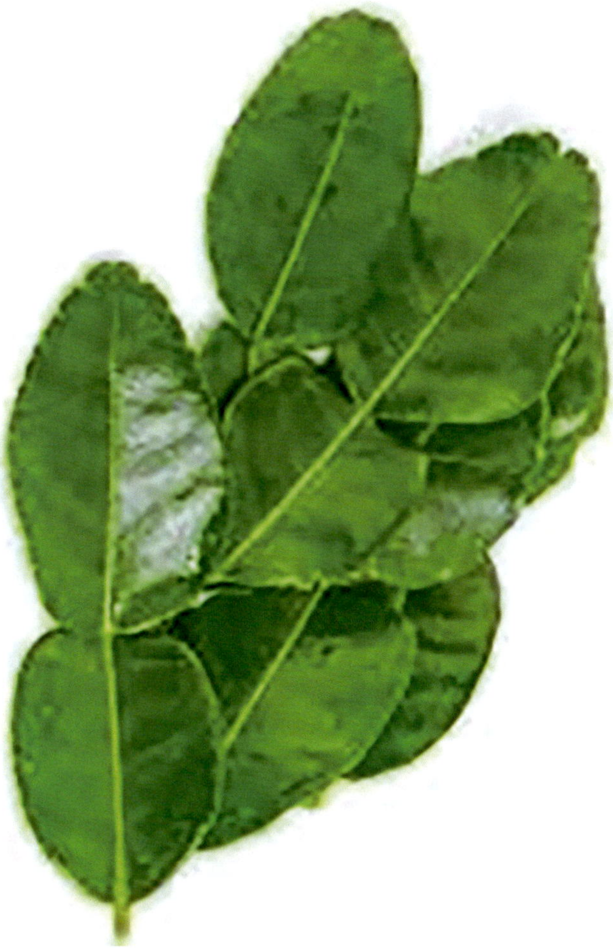

Lavender

Recipe 42

Lemon Madeleines with Lavender

Once lavender is in bloom, I rush to collect handfuls and prepare these delicate treats.

Snack – Teatime
Makes 24 madeleines
Prep time: 40 minutes
Cooking time: 7 to 8 minutes

Ingredients

175g/three quarter cup unsalted butter, melted, plus more for the baking pans
375g/14 oz. cake flour, sifted (not self-rising)
1/2tsp baking powder
1/4tsp coarse salt
3 large eggs plus 2 large egg yolks
175g/three quarter cup granulated sugar
2tbs finely grated lemon zest
2tbs fresh lemon juice
2tbs edible (untreated) lavender petals. (Ask your grocer or florist.)

Method

Preheat oven to 200°C/400°F. Butter two madeleine pans. Set aside.
Sift flour, baking powder, and salt into a bowl; set aside.
Put eggs, egg yolks, granulated sugar, and lemon zest and juice into the bowl of an electric mixer fitted with the paddle attachment. Mix on medium-high speed until pale and thickened in about 5 minutes. Mix in the butter and lavender petals. Using a spatula, fold flour mixture into egg mixture. Let rest 30 minutes.
Pour batter into buttered pans, filling the moulds 3/4 full. Bake for 7 to 8 minutes, until edges are crisp and golden. Let the madeleines cool slightly in the pans. Invert, unmould, and serve on one of your prettiest dessert dishes.

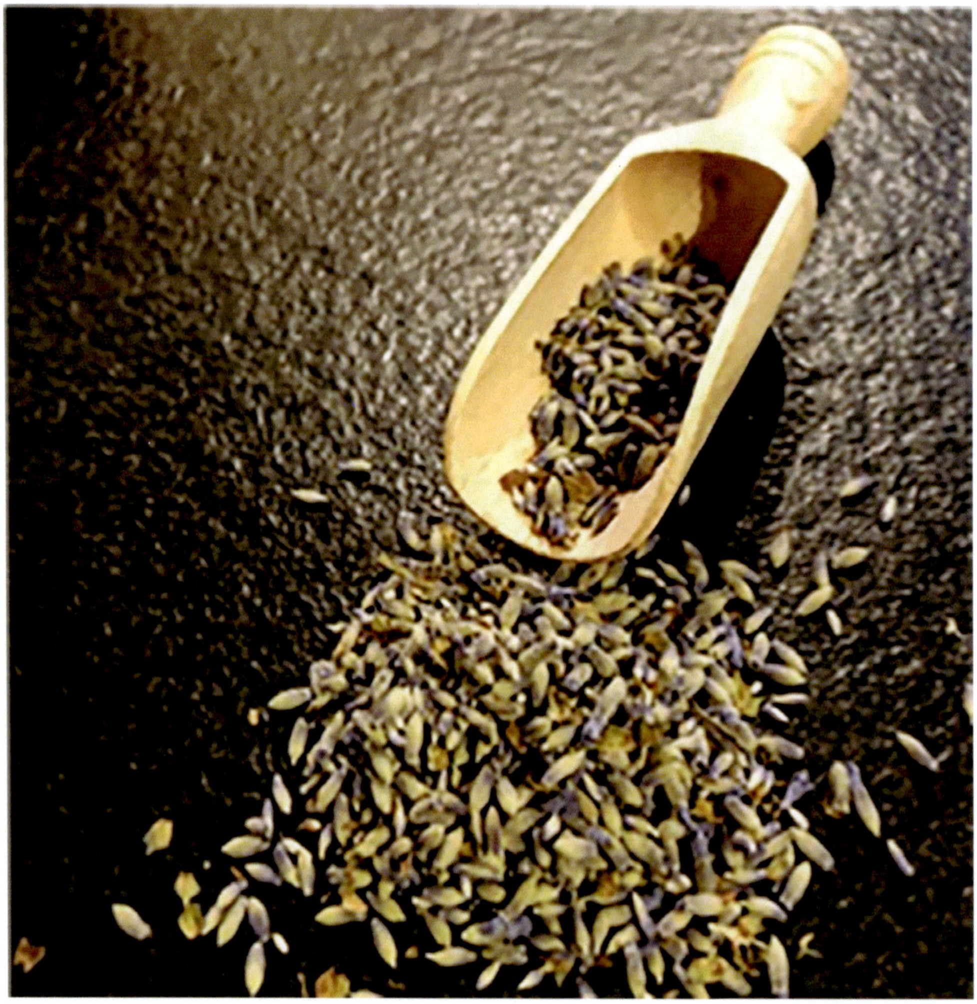

Lemongrass

Recipe 43

Nam Manao – Limeade with Lemongrass

Refreshing, thirst-quenching, and a real crowd-pleaser

Beverage
Serves 2
Preparation time: 20minutes
Chilling time: 60 minutes

Ingredients

250ml/1 cup freshly squeezed lime juice, reserve rinds
3 stalks of lemongrass, sliced thinly
Half a liter/2 cups water
250g/half cup sugar
1 pinch of salt
Soda water (to top up the glasses and add some fizz)
Lime slices and lemongrass stalks to garnish
Ice cubes

Method

In a saucepan, heat the water to a boil. Add the sugar and salt. Stir to dissolve. Take the pan off the heat. Add the lemongrass and the lime rinds and allow to steep for 15 minutes.

Strain and pour the liquid into a pitcher.

Add the lime juice, stir, and refrigerate until ready to serve.

Pour the limeade into cocktail glasses over plenty of ice, filling 3/4 of the way. Top up with the soda water and garnish with lime slices and a lemongrass stalk.

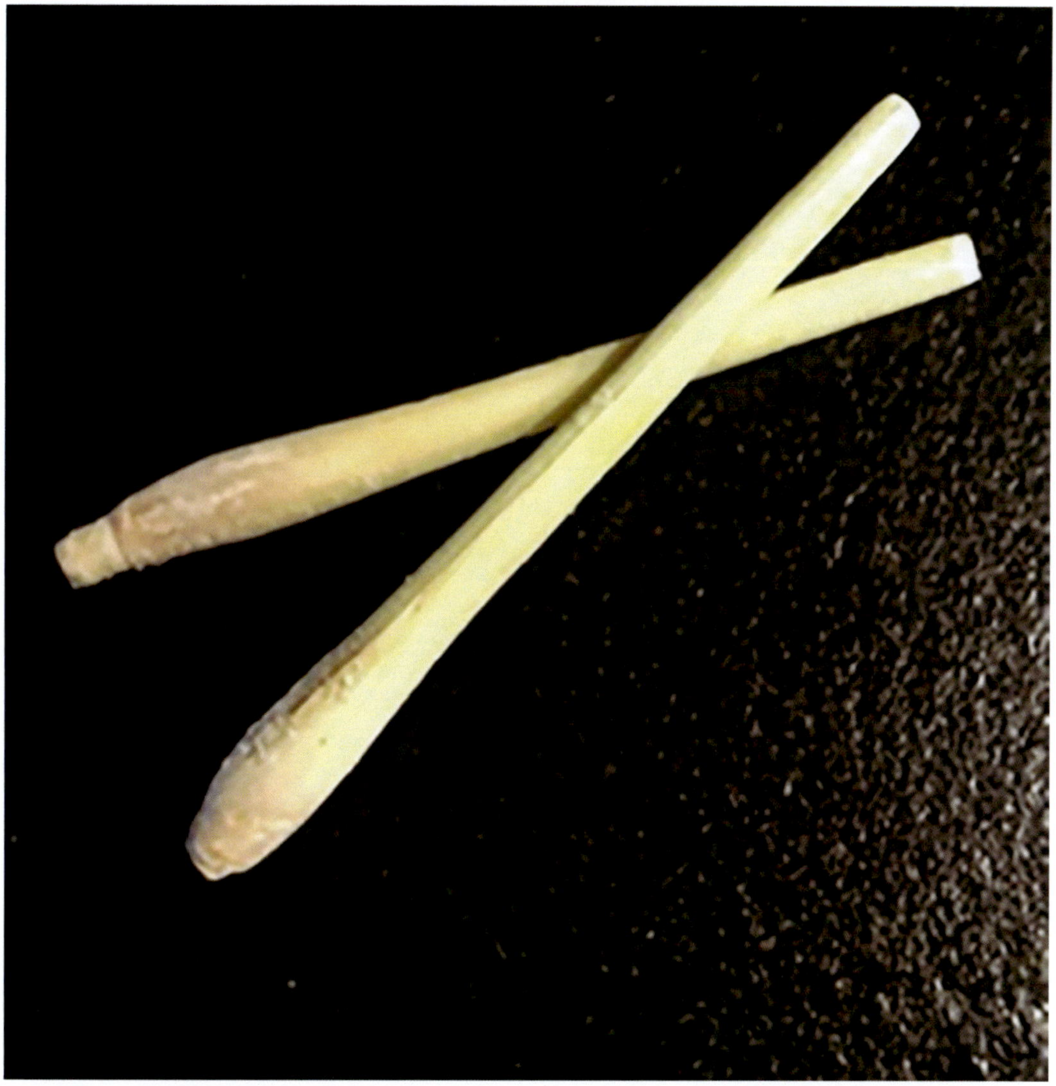

Lemongrass

Recipe 44

Linden Leaf Tea

A calming tea for any time of the year

In June, when the Linden tree is in bloom, pick some of the pale green leaves together with the flowers. Spread the leaves and flowers on to a wooden board and keep in the driest part of your home for a couple of days. Then put the partially dried leaves and flowers into a paper bag for about one week. Once the leaves and flowers are nice and dry, pack them into a clean glass jar.

Take a handful and brew a cup of linden leaf tea whenever you wish.

Marjoram

Recipe 45

Sweet Sautéed Carrots with Orange and Marjoram

A lovely complement to a Sunday roast

Side dish
Serves 4
Prep time: 7 minutes
Cooking time: 10 to 12 minutes

Ingredients

3tbs olive oil
16 carrots cut, on the diagonal, into 4cm slices
1tsp honey
1tbs orange marmalade
1/2tsp freshly ground black pepper
2 pinches of salt
1tbs dried marjoram
1tbs fresh marjoram
1tbs fresh orange juice
2tbs Grand Marnier

Method

In a medium non-stick sauté pan, heat 1 to 2tbs of the oil over moderately low heat. Add the carrots, honey, orange marmalade, salt, pepper, and the dried marjoram. Cook, covered, stirring occasionally for 5 minutes.

Uncover the pan. Raise the heat to moderate and cook, stirring frequently, until the carrots are very tender and start to brown, about 8 minutes longer.

Pour the Grand Marnier and carefully light, allowing the alcohol to burn off.

Remove the pan from the heat. Stir in the remaining 1 to 2 tablespoons of oil and the orange juice. Place in a serving bowl. Pour over the pan juices and sprinkle the fresh marjoram.

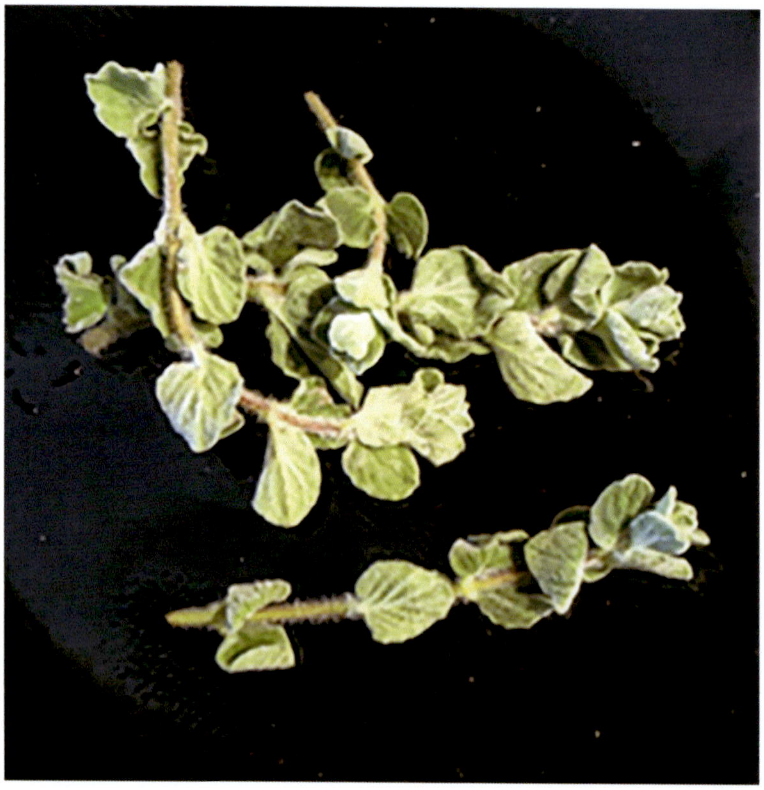

Mint

Recipe 46

Mojito

Mojito memory: sipping my first (ever) at the Sunset Pier, Key West, FL while watching the sunset = CHEERS!

Apéro
Serves 2

Ingredients

60ml/quarter cup lime juice
20 mint leaves
120ml/half cup white rum
30ml/eighth cup sugar syrup
Top up with tonic to give it fizz.

Method

Divide the mint between 2 cocktail glasses and crush them with the back of a wooden spoon to release the mint oil from the leaves.

In a cocktail shaker filled with ice, pour in the sugar syrup, lime juice, and rum. Shake until the sides of the shaker become frosty.

Pour into the glasses and top up with tonic.

Garnish with sliced lime, mint, and (if you can find it) sugarcane.

Mint

Recipe 47

Orange and Pineapple with Mint Sugar

Quick, easy, and deliciously fresh!

Dessert
Serves 6
Prep time: 10 minutes
Gluten-free
Dairy-free

Ingredients

4 oranges, peeled and sliced
1 pineapple, sliced and cut into chunks
4 tablespoons of mint leaves
4 tablespoons of caster sugar
1 lime
Pinch of salt

Method

Arrange the fruit on a serving platter or on individual dessert plates.
Squeeze the lime over the fruit.
Mince the mint leaves until very fine and mix with the sugar (A mini food processor makes short work of this step.) and the pinch of salt.
Sprinkle this mint sugar over the fruit and serve.

Mustard seeds

Recipe 48

Piquant Potatoes

Indian flavours to spice up some spuds

Side Dish
Serves 4
Prep time: 20 minutes
Cooking time: 15 minutes
Gluten-free

Also see video on my YouTube channel: lockedintastes

Ingredients

750g/pound and half potatoes, (Waxy or all-purpose) peeled and cut into cubes
Drizzle of olive oil
3tsp black or white mustard seeds
1tsp cumin seeds
1tsp freshly ground black pepper
1 bunch of coriander, chopped
1 freshly squeezed lemon
Pinch of salt

Method

Peel and quarter the potatoes and boil in salted water until they're tender, then drain and dry.

Heat a drizzle of olive in a nonstick frying pan and, when it's hot, add the cumin and mustard seeds and wait a moment until they start to pop.

Quickly add the potatoes and stir until they start to brown at the edges. Then add the black pepper and two pinches of salt.

Keep stirring and frying until the potatoes are nicely browned and a bit crispy on the edges.

Toss in the coriander, stir, and then squeeze the lemon juice. Stir again and serve hot

Nigella seeds

Recipe 49

Mango Chutney

Serve with your favourite Indian curry or tandoori. It is also delicious with raclette.

Makes about 4 small glass jars
Cook time: 60 minutes
Preserving time: 30 minutes

Ingredients

4tbs fresh ginger, finely grated
2 red chilis, sliced
2tsp whole nigella seeds
1tsp ground coriander
1tsp ground cumin
1tsp turmeric powder
10 toasted cardamom seeds
5 whole cloves
1tsp ground cinnamon and 2 whole cinnamon sticks
Half tsp salt
4 to 5 mangoes (about 250g/8 oz. each), peeled and diced
500g/2 cups white granulated sugar
175ml/three quarter cup white vinegar

Method

In a large saucepan, sauté the ginger and red chilies in a little water for a minute. Add the spices and sauté for another minute. Add the diced mangoes, sugar, salt, and vinegar and stir to combine. Bring to a rapid boil and then reduce to medium-low heat. Steady simmer for 45 minutes. Remove from heat and allow to cool.

Storage

The chutney will stay in the fridge for approximately 6 weeks, but for a longer shelf-life, you may prefer to pour the hot mixture directly into sterilised jars and boil the jars in a water bath, submerging the glass jar completely for 15 minutes.

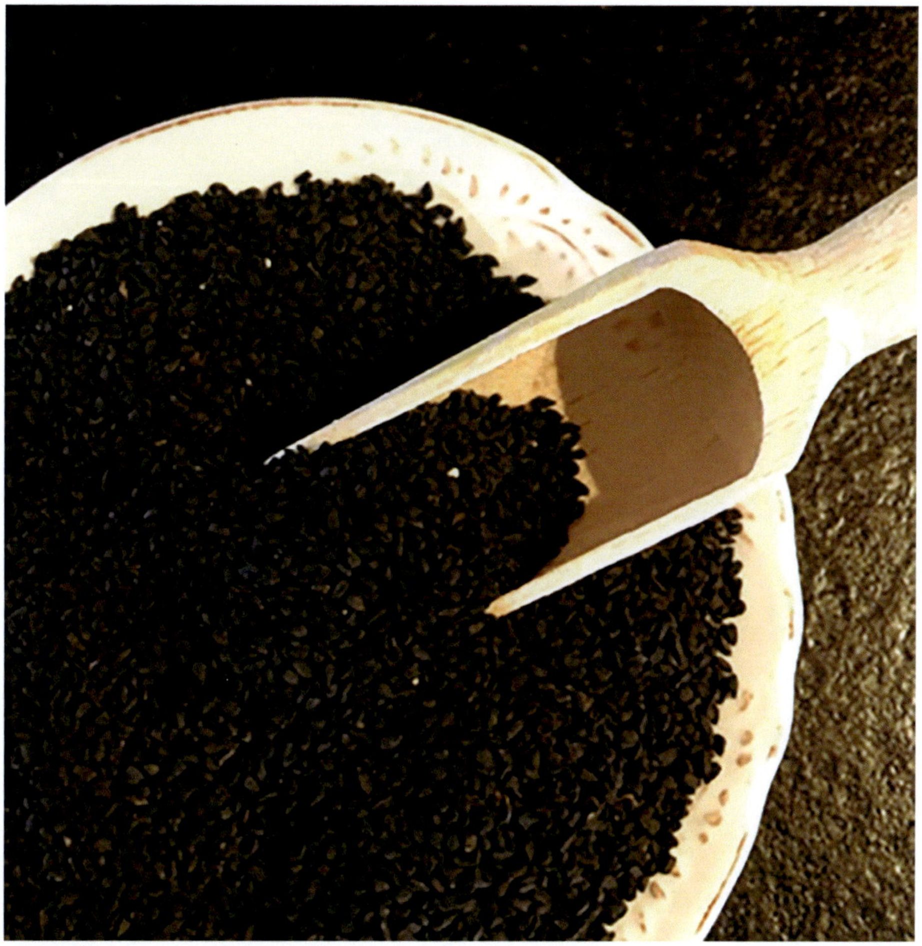

Nigella seeds

Recipe 50

Raita

A lovely way to cool down a fiery curry

Starter or Side Dish
Servings 4
Prep time: 15 minutes
Chill time: 2 hours

Ingredients

1 large cucumber
500g/2 cups plain yogurt
1tbs nigella seeds
1tbs ground cumin seeds
1/2tsp ground coriander seeds
1/2tsp salt
1/2tsp sugar
1/4tsp cayenne
Juice of 1 lemon
1 bunch of mint, chopped

Method

Slice the cucumber in half. Use a spoon to scrape out the seeds and discard them.

Then grate the half cucumbers onto a kitchen towel. This will remove the excess moisture. Set aside.

In a bowl, stir together the yogurt, cumin, coriander, cayenne, lemon juice, sugar, salt, and pepper. Add the cucumber and stir to combine. Then stir in the mint. Taste and adjust the seasoning as you wish.

Cover and refrigerate for a couple of hours to allow the flavours to combine.

Top with the nigella seeds and serve as a starter with poppadums or to accompany your favourite Indian curry

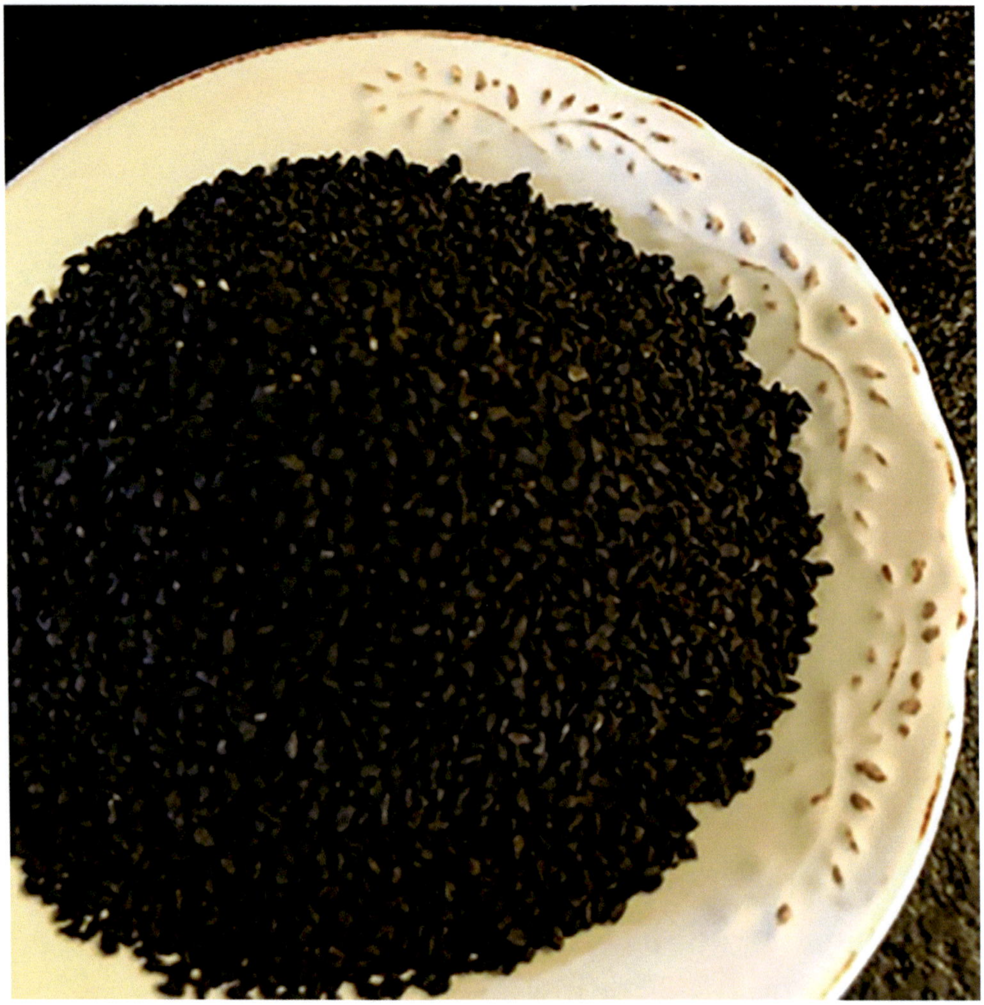

Nutmeg

Recipe 51

Chestnut Gnocchi with Gorgonzola and Pear

An autumn favourite from Northern Italy

Primo Piatto
Serves 8
Prep Time: 2 hours
Cooking Time: 10 minutes
Gluten-free

Ingredients
For the Gnocchi

4 large floury-type potatoes
400g/14 oz. chestnut flour, and some more for dusting
225g/1 cup ricotta cheese
1 large egg
1tsp salt

For the Gorgonzola and Pear Sauce

2tbs butter
2 firm but ripe pears
225ml/1 cup heavy cream
1tbs brandy or cream sherry
200g/7 oz. Gorgonzola cheese

To serve

Pinches of nutmeg
Sprigs of fresh thyme

Method
Making the gnocchi

    Scrub and wash the potatoes and place in large pot of boiling water. Cook for about 20 minutes with salt until fork-tender. Remove from water and place in a colander to cool and drain.
    Peel the potatoes when cool. Then finely grate them using a box grater, or a rice mill, on to a baking tray lined with baking paper and place into a warm oven at 100°C/200°F to 'dry' for half an hour.
    Form the potatoes into a mound on a large work surface. Pile the chestnut flour on top. Sprinkle salt around the base of the mound.
    Make a hole in the middle of the mound, creating a 'well.' Crack the egg

into the well and add the ricotta. Blend these with your hands, from out to in, to make a dough. Knead the dough only enough to incorporate all the ingredients. Form the dough into a fat log shape. Cut the fat log into 8 pieces. Dust with flour as you shape each piece into a rope by rolling with your hands. Do not over-flour. The rope should have about the width of your middle finger.

Then slice the rope into bite-sized pieces. Roll the back of a fork over the gnocchi, flicking each into a curl-shape and set aside.

Start your sauce while heating the salted water for cooking the gnocchi.

Gorgonzola and Pear Sauce

Remove skin and core from pears. Chop into small bite-size pieces.

Melt butter over medium high heat in a heavy-bottom sauté pan. Add pears and brown slightly for about 3 minutes. Don't overcook.

Remove pan from hob. Add brandy or cream sherry. Gently swirl pan to incorporate cognac for 30 seconds. Return to heat.

Add gorgonzola. Let the cheese melt before adding milk, cream, and nutmeg. Keep simmering on low heat. The sauce will thicken slightly while you start boiling your gnocchi.

Boiling the Gnocchi

Gently shake the flour off the gnocchi and drop them into the boiling water. Don't overcrowd the pan. It will take a few batches.

When the gnocchi rise to the surface, remove them with a slotted spoon and drain on towel.

To Serve

Once cooked, place the gnocchi in serving bowls, pour over the sauce, add the obligatory pinch of nutmeg, and garnish with a sprig of thyme.

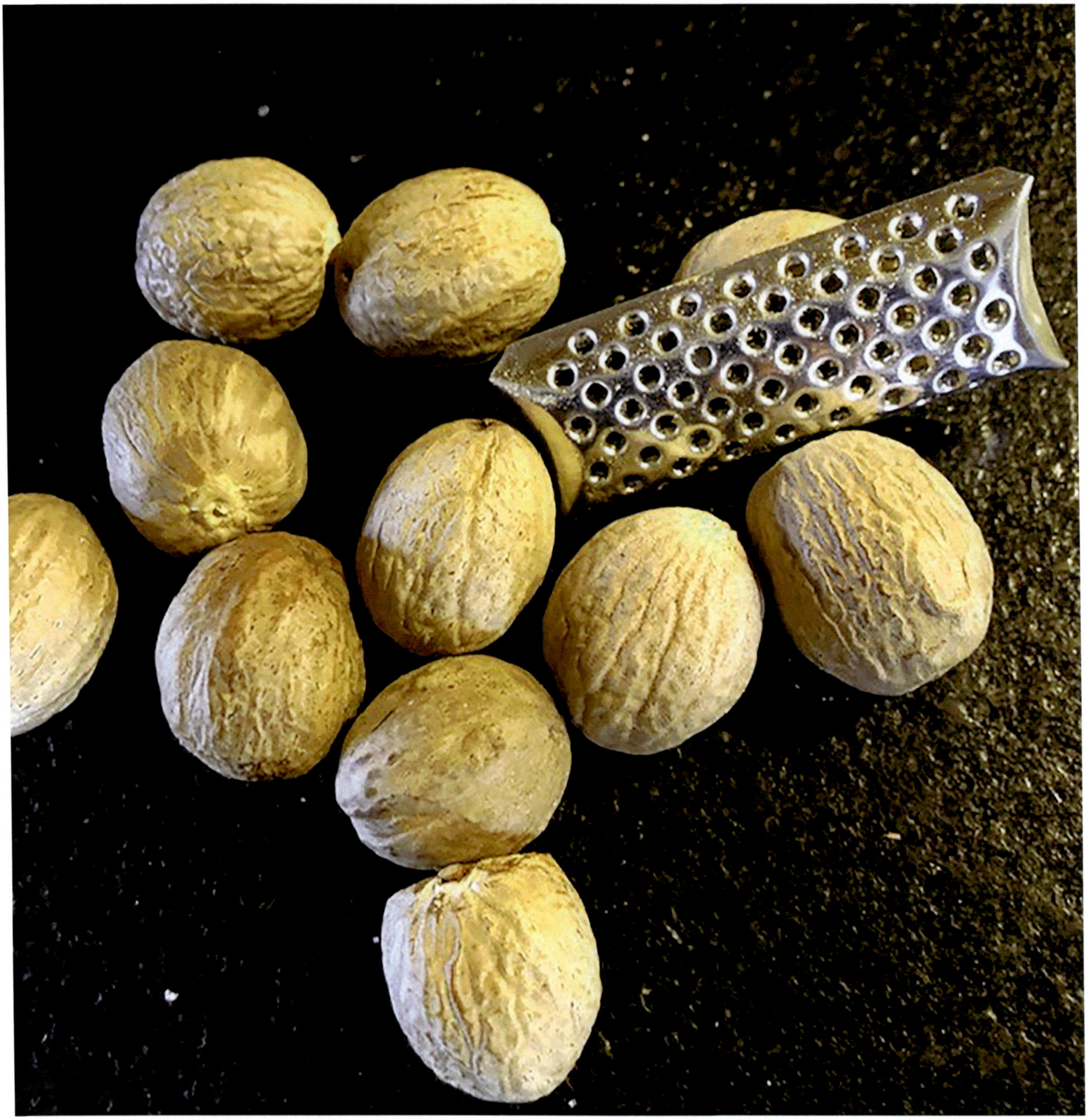

Nutmeg

Recipe 52

Gratinato di Finocchio con Noce Moscata (Fennel Gratin with Nutmeg)

A flavourful accompaniment to a Sunday roast or a baked fish dinner

Side dish
4 servings
Prep time: 20 minutes
Baking time: 30 minutes
Gluten-free

Ingredients

3 bulbs of fennel, sliced
3tbs butter
125ml/1 cup cream
125g/8 oz. gorgonzola cheese
125g/1 cup breadcrumbs, gluten-free preferred
125g parmesan cheese, grated
1tbs nutmeg, freshly grated
1tsp salt

Method

In a large saucepan, add 1 liter/2 cups of water and salt and bring to boil. Add the fennel and reduce the heat to medium. Boil the fennel until fairly tender (about 10 minutes). Drain and set aside.

Preheat the oven to 180°C/350°F. Butter a large ovenproof baking dish or individual baking dishes.

Using the large saucepan again, melt 2tbs of butter. Then add the cream, gorgonzola cheese and stir. Turn off the heat. Add the fennel and stir until the mixture is creamy and well combined

Spoon the fennel mixture into the baking dishes.

In a separate bowl, mix the breadcrumbs and parmesan cheese together.

Sprinkle the breadcrumb mixture over the fennel and grate the nutmeg, using a nutmeg grater, over the top. Dab the remaining 1tbs of butter on top of the breadcrumb topping.

Bake for 30 minutes and serve HOT.

Orange blossom water

Recipe 53

Sicilian Blood Orange and Fennel Salad

The fresh taste of Sicily in the form of a crisp salad to serve especially with your favourite fish or seafood recipes

Side dish
Serves 4
Prep time: 15 minutes
Chilling time: 60 minutes
Dairy-free

Ingredients

2 large blood oranges (or, if not available, navel oranges), peeled, pith removed, and sliced
1 large bulb of fennel, sliced
1tbs of very thinly sliced red onions
3tbs extra virgin olive oil
2tbs of orange blossom water
Mint leaves, torn
2tbs crushed pistachios (optional)
Salt and pepper to taste

Method

Toss the orange and fennel together in a large bowl. Add the orange blossom water and olive oil and toss again. Add salt and pepper to taste.

Cover with cling film and chill for 1 hour.

Sprinkle the crushed pistachios and add freshly ground pepper and salt to taste.

Serve with torn mint leaves.

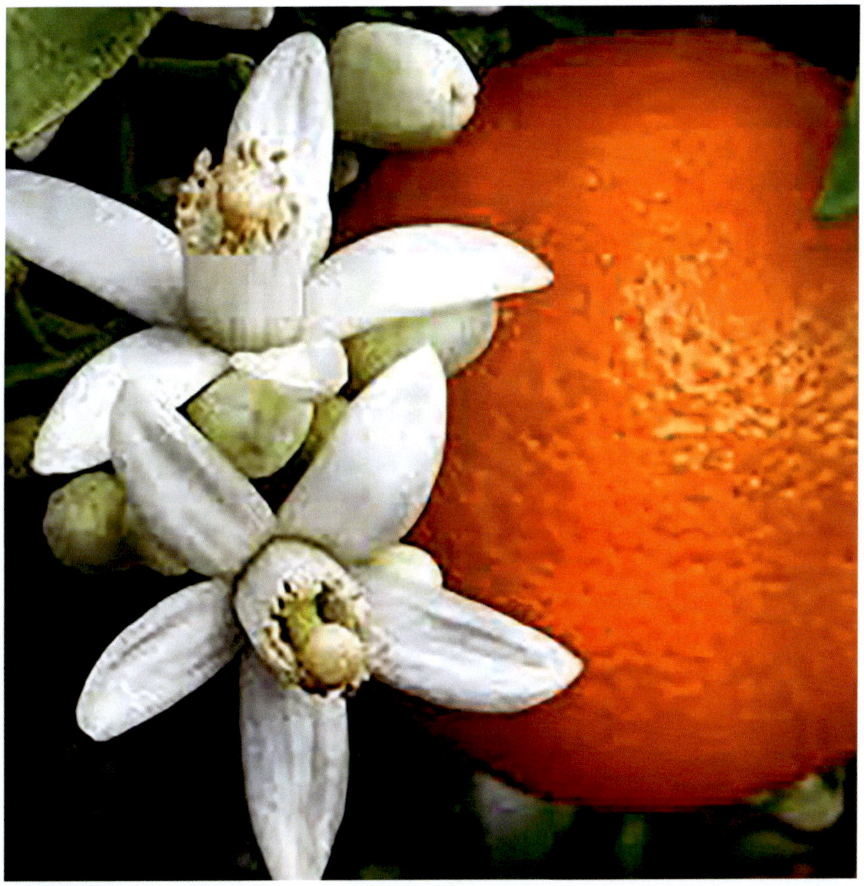

Orange blossom water

Recipe 54

Ramos Gin Fizz

Inspired by Henry C. Ramos who invented this version at his bar, the Imperial Cabinet Saloon, in New Orleans in 1888. It remains a fab way to cool down on a hot summer's day.

Apéro
Serves 1
Gluten-free

Ingredients

1tbs fresh lime juice
1tbs fresh lemon juice
60ml/2fl oz. gin
30ml/1fl oz. sugar syrup
1tbs single cream
1 egg white
1tsp orange blossom water
Top up with soda water
Slice of fresh orange for garnish

Method

Shake all ingredients, except for the soda water in a cocktail shaker filled with ice until the outside of the shaker becomes frosty (about 30 seconds).
Pour into a highball glass. Top up with soda water and serve with a slice of fresh orange.

Oregano

Recipe 55

Baked Aubergine with Tomatoes and Feta

A super-satisfying and easy casserole to prepare at any time of the year

Serves: 6 as a side dish or…
4 as a main course
Prep time: 10 minutes
Cooking time: 30 minutes
Gluten-free

Ingredients

2 medium aubergines, peeled and chopped into cubes
500g/2 cups tinned chopped tomatoes and their juice 250g/1 cup feta cheese cut into cubes
2tbs of fresh oregano (or dried if fresh not available)
Olive oil to drizzle
60g/quarter cup breadcrumbs or (even better) pine-nuts, to create a crunchy topping

Method

Preheat oven to 180°C/350°F.
Drizzle olive oil in the bottom of a rectangular baking dish.
Add the aubergine cubes and toss with the olive oil.
Layer the tinned chopped tomatoes over the aubergine cubes and then the feta cheese. Sprinkle the breadcrumbs (or pine-nuts) and oregano on top.
Drizzle a little more of olive oil and bake for 30 minutes.

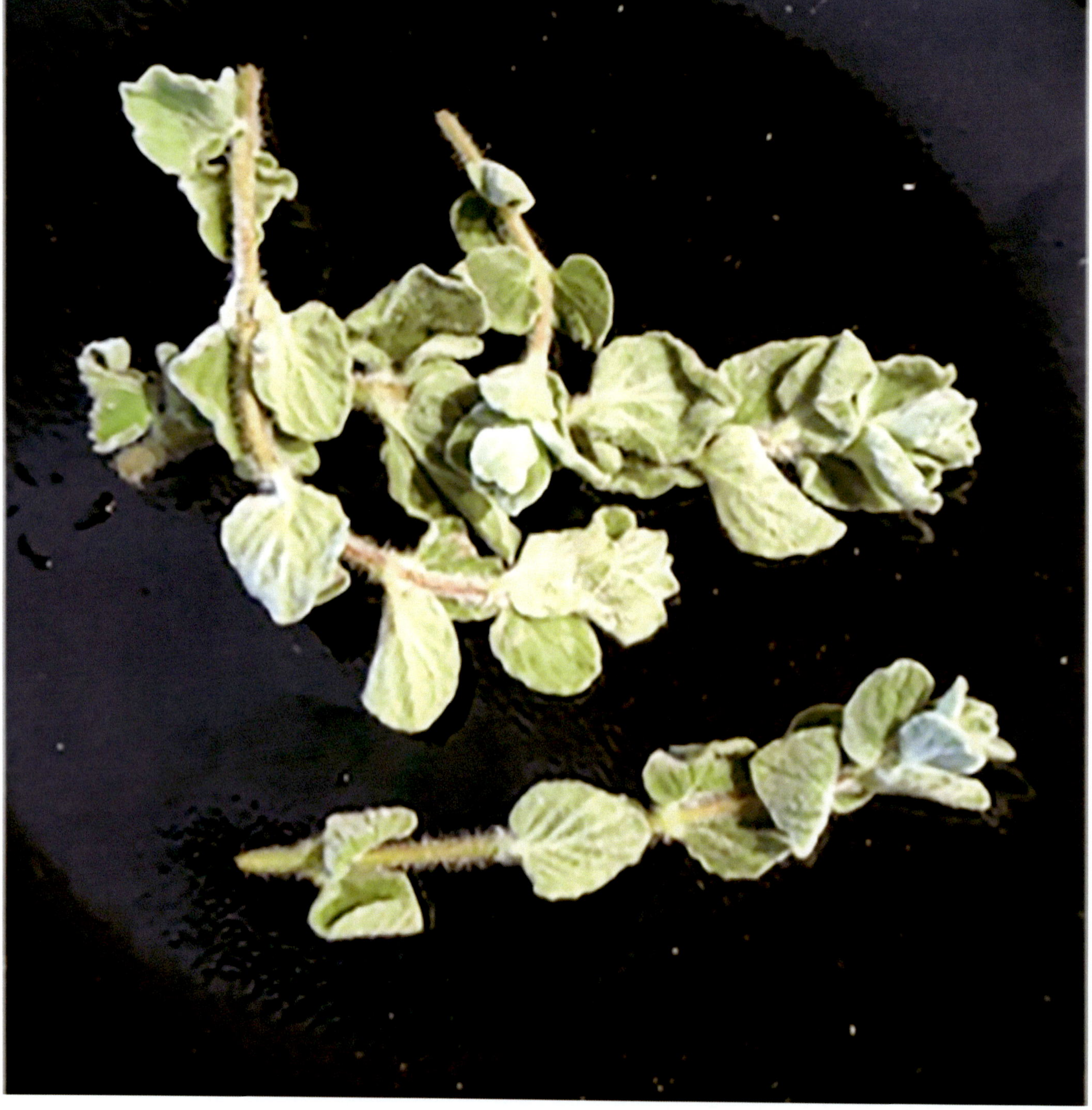

Oregano

Recipe 56

Roast Rack of Lamb

A British and Australian favourite, but my Mediterranean version is how we make it at home.

Main course
Serves 4
Prep time: 60 minutes
Cooking time: 12 minutes
Gluten-free
Dairy-free

Ingredients

2 racks of lamb (8 ribs each), trimmed
2 lemons
1tbs freshly cracked pepper
1tbs salt
Handful of fresh oregano, pulsed, or 1tbs of dried
250ml/1 cup olive oil
Crema di balsamico: a drizzle

Method

Separate the racks with a sharp pointed knife, counting 2 chops per cut, and place into a re-sealable plastic bag. Pour in 250ml/1 cup of olive oil and marinate in the refrigerator for 12 hours. This olive oil trick creates just the most luscious tender chops.

Remove from the plastic bag, drain off the oil, and place in a shallow roasting pan.

Squeeze the lemon juice over the lamb and place the lemon rinds into the pan.

Season with salt and pepper. Toss the oregano on top and leave to rest for one hour.

Preheat the oven to 220°C/425°F

Cook the lamb. For medium-rare, 6 minutes on each side.

Serve with roasted potatoes, grilled vegetables, and a drizzle crema di balsamico.

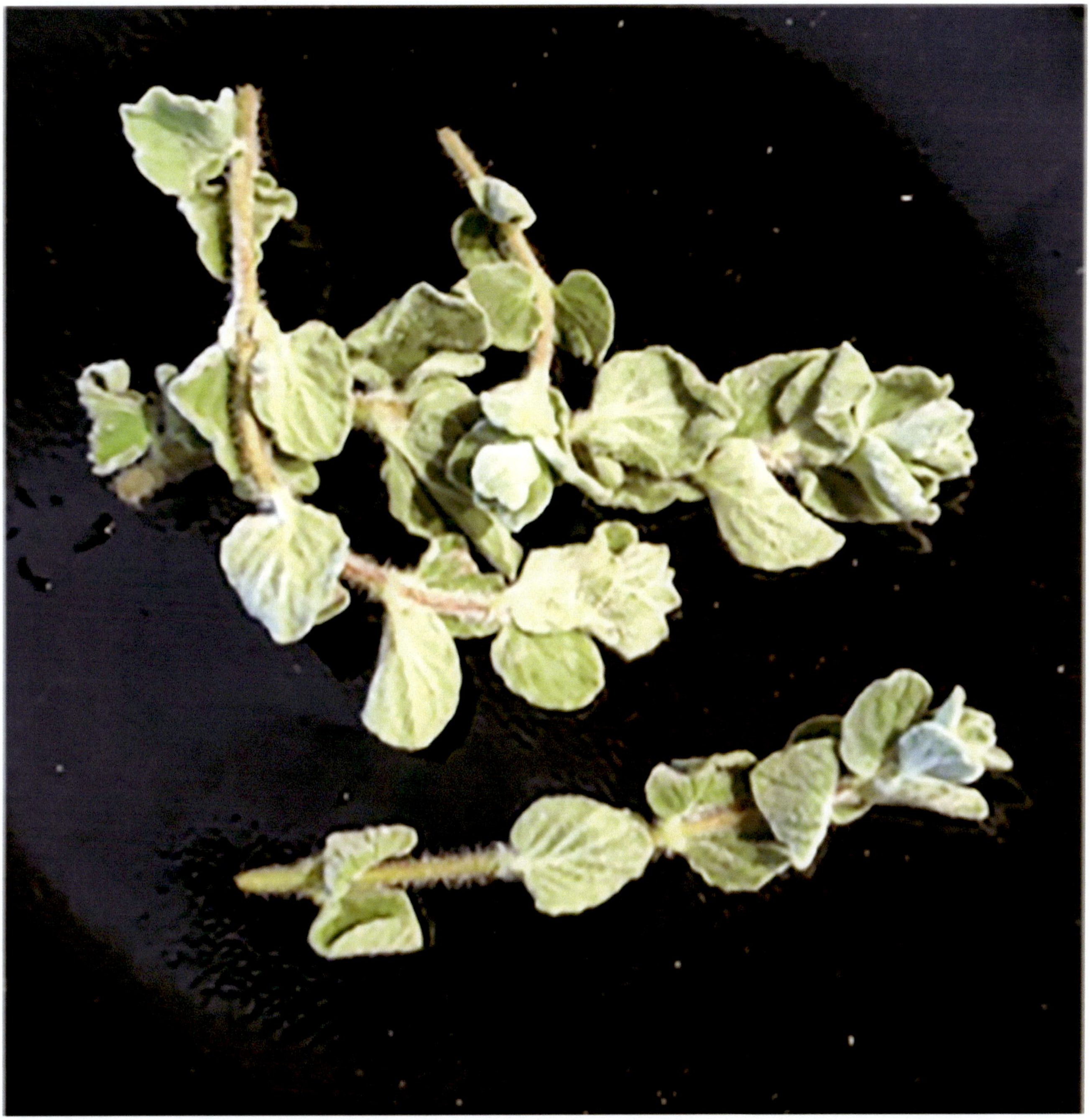

Pandan leaves

Recipe 57

Pandan Juice

A mainstay for Southeast Asian desserts, and tastier if you make your own. (Recipe inspired by Anita Jacobson)

Sauce
Prep Time: 15 minutes
Total Time: 15 minutes
Makes 125ml of pandan juice

Ingredients

18 fresh or frozen pandan leaves
125ml/half cup water

Method

Rinse the leaves. Then with a pair of scissors, cut the leaves into pieces and fill a blender with them.
Add water and blend. Continue blending until the leaves are reduced to tiny bits.
Use a strainer or sieve to strain.
Transfer the pandan juice into a sterilised glass jar.
Store refrigerated for up to one week.

Pandan leaves

Recipe 58

Pandan Coconut Ice Cream

Taste of faraway lands where being green is definitely cool!

Dessert
Serves 4
Prep and cooking time: 30 minutes
Chilling time: 4 to 6 hours
Gluten-free
Dairy-free
Vegan

Ingredients

250ml/1 cup coconut cream
400ml/14fl oz. full-fat coconut milk
8tbs pandan juice (See Pandan Juice: Recipe 57.)
120g/half cup sugar, adjusted to the sweetness of your tooth
Pinch of salt

Method

Place all ingredients into a medium-sized saucepan and bring to a rapid boil. Then lower the temperature to simmer and cook for 10 minutes to create a custard.

Pour the custard into an ice cream maker and follow the machine-manufacturer's instructions.

If you do not have an ice cream maker, no worries; simply pour your custard into a plastic container and place in the freezer. After 1 hour, the custard will start to form crystals. Gently stir the custard from time to time and continue to check it every hour and, in 4 to 6 hours, your ice cream will be ready to serve.

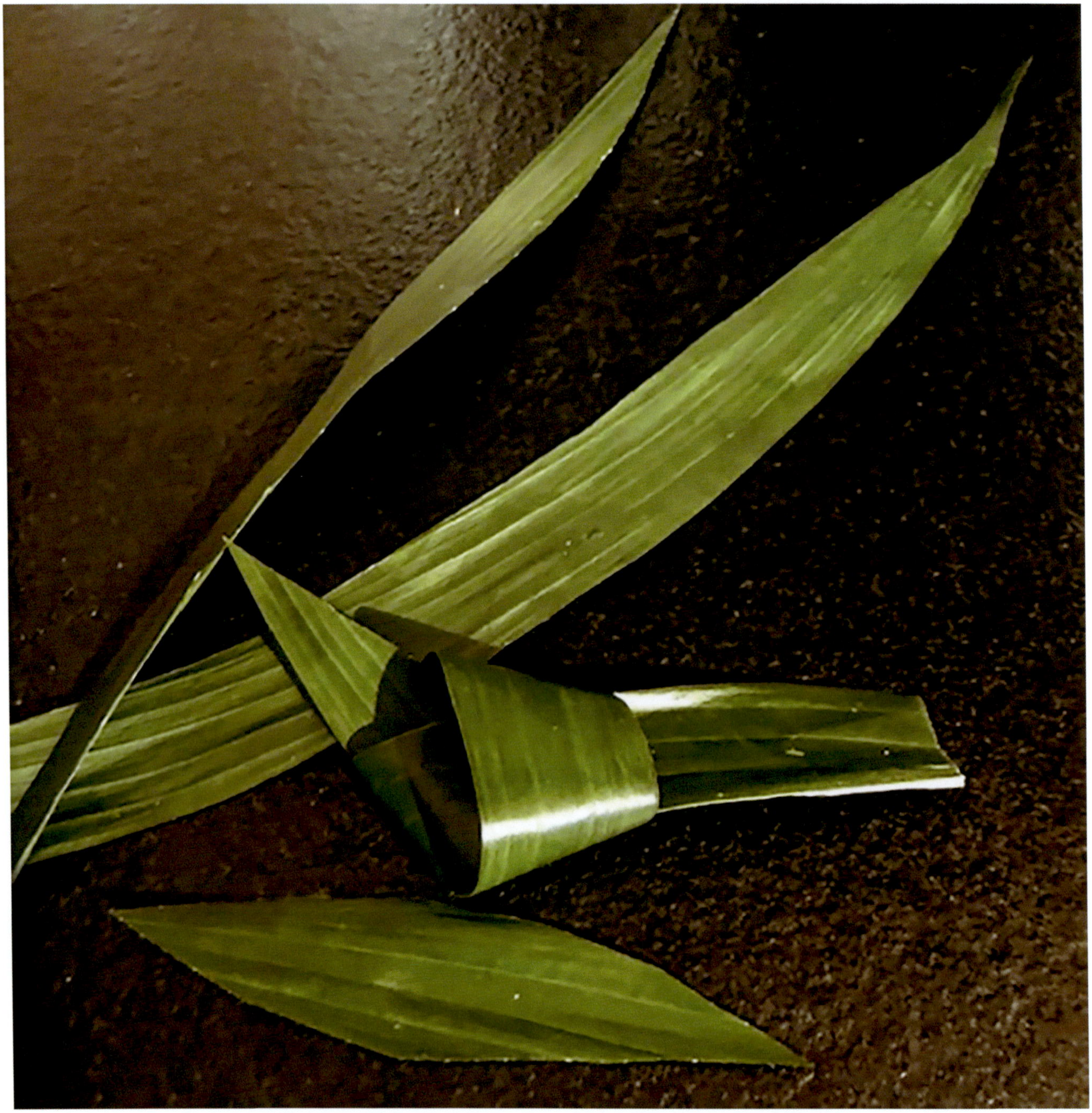

Paprika

Recipe 59

Sandra's Roasted Potatoes

Potatoes that work with every dish, every day, at any time.

Side dish
Serves 4 to 6
Prep time: 25 minutes
Cook time: 45 minutes
Gluten-free

Also see video on my YouTube channel: lockedintastes

Ingredients

1kg/2lbs floury potatoes, such as King Edward or Maris Piper, peeled and chopped into cubes
1tbs salt
2tbs paprika
2tbs butter, cubed
2tbs olive oil
Sprigs of fresh rosemary and sage
Salt and pepper to taste

Method

Preheat the oven to 180°C/350°F.
Boil the potatoes in a large saucepan with 1tbs salt until tender. Drain and place on to a baking tray. Drizzle olive oil and drop pieces of butter on to the potatoes. Sprinkle the paprika and roast for 45 minutes or until the potatoes are well roasted and crispy.
Add salt and pepper to taste.
Serve with sprigs of fresh rosemary and sage.

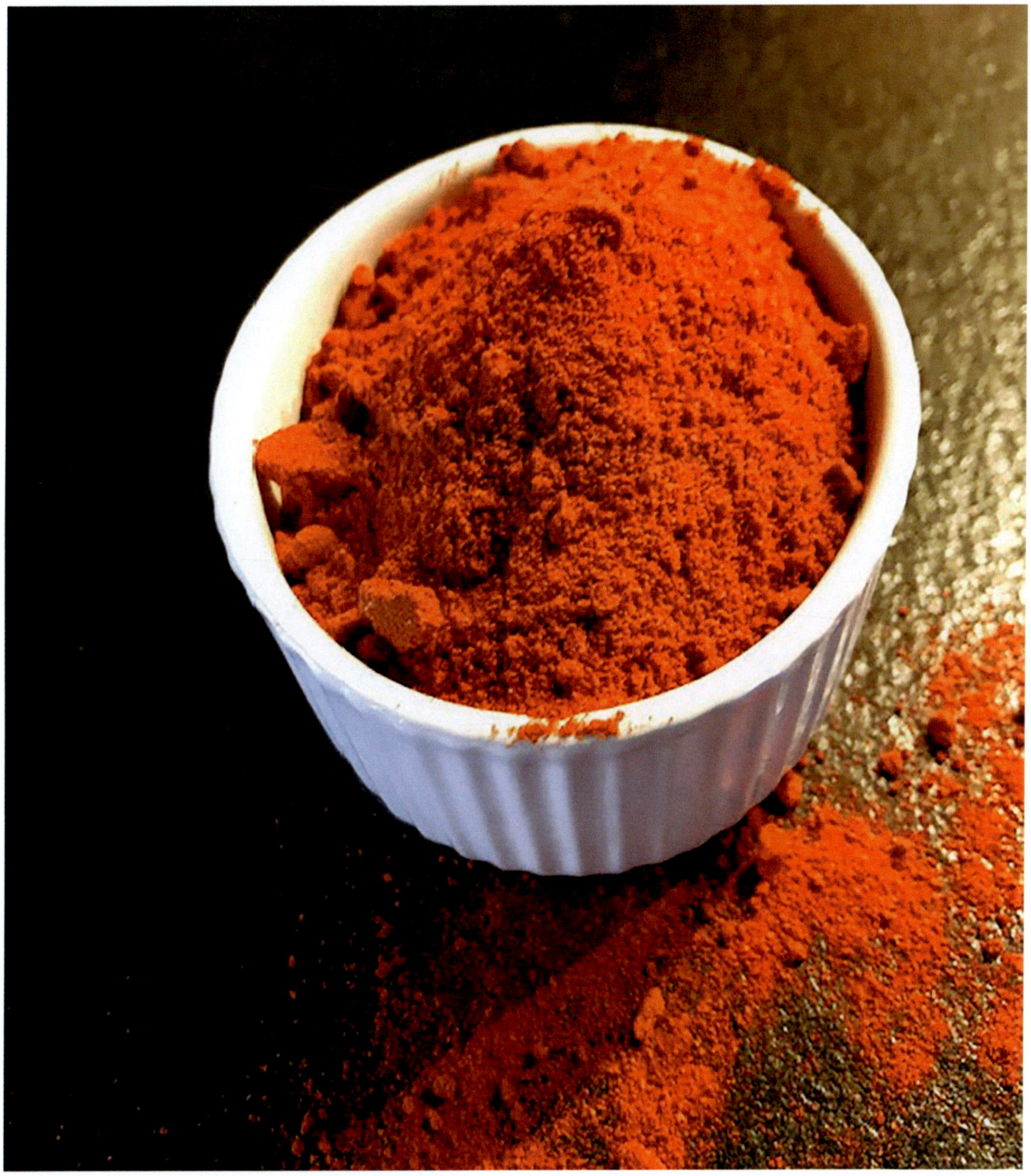

Parsley

Recipe 60

Carciofi (Artichokes) Alla Romana

In springtime, keep your eyes open for mammola or cimarolo artichokes (medium-sized globe artichokes). These beauties are perfect for this traditional Roman specialty.

Starter
Serves 4
Prep time: 20 minutes
Cooking time: 30 to 40 minutes
Gluten-free
Dairy-free

Ingredients

4 globe artichokes
3 lemons, quartered
1 bunch of flat-leaf parsley, chopped
250ml/1cup vegetable stock
250ml/1cup dry white wine
120ml/half cup olive oil
Salt and pepper

Method

Cut the tip off of the artichokes (about the top third). Rub the cut surfaces with the lemon to prevent them from turning brown.

Peel the tough outer covering of the stem to reveal the white flesh underneath. Snap off the leathery outer leaves to expose the tender light green leaves beneath. And trim with a knife the dark green parts around the base of the artichoke. The size of the artichokes will be vastly reduced – don't worry; you are creating a melt-in-your-mouth experience!

From the top of each artichoke, reach down with your fingers to expose the prickly, thorny choke (toward the bottom of the globe) and remove it carefully with a small knife.

Rub the cut surfaces with the lemon quarters. Now drop the trimmed artichokes into a bowl of water with the juice of half a lemon to prevent browning. Reserve the squeezed lemon sections for cooking.

In a separate bowl, mix the chopped parsley, salt, pepper, and the juice from one lemon.

Remove the artichokes from their bowl and dry with a kitchen towel. Rub the parsley and salt mixture into the leaves and crevices of the artichokes.

Pour olive oil into a casserole and heat to a simmer.

Place the artichokes, top side down/stems pointing up and arrange the squeezed lemon halves around the artichokes.

Add the vegetable stock and the white wine. The liquid should reach half way up the artichokes.

Cover and cook over medium heat until the artichokes are cooked through (approx. 30 to 40 minutes). To test, poke a knife through the centre of an artichoke to see if it is tender. You may need to add more stock during the cooking process to make up for some evaporation. The liquid will become a flavourful reduced sauce.

Let the artichokes cool in the sauce to room temperature.

Place each artichoke into a shallow serving bowl. Spoon over the sauce and garnish with chopped parsley and a lemon wedge. Serve with extra virgin olive oil (to drizzle) and chunks of crusty bread for dipping into the tasty sauce.

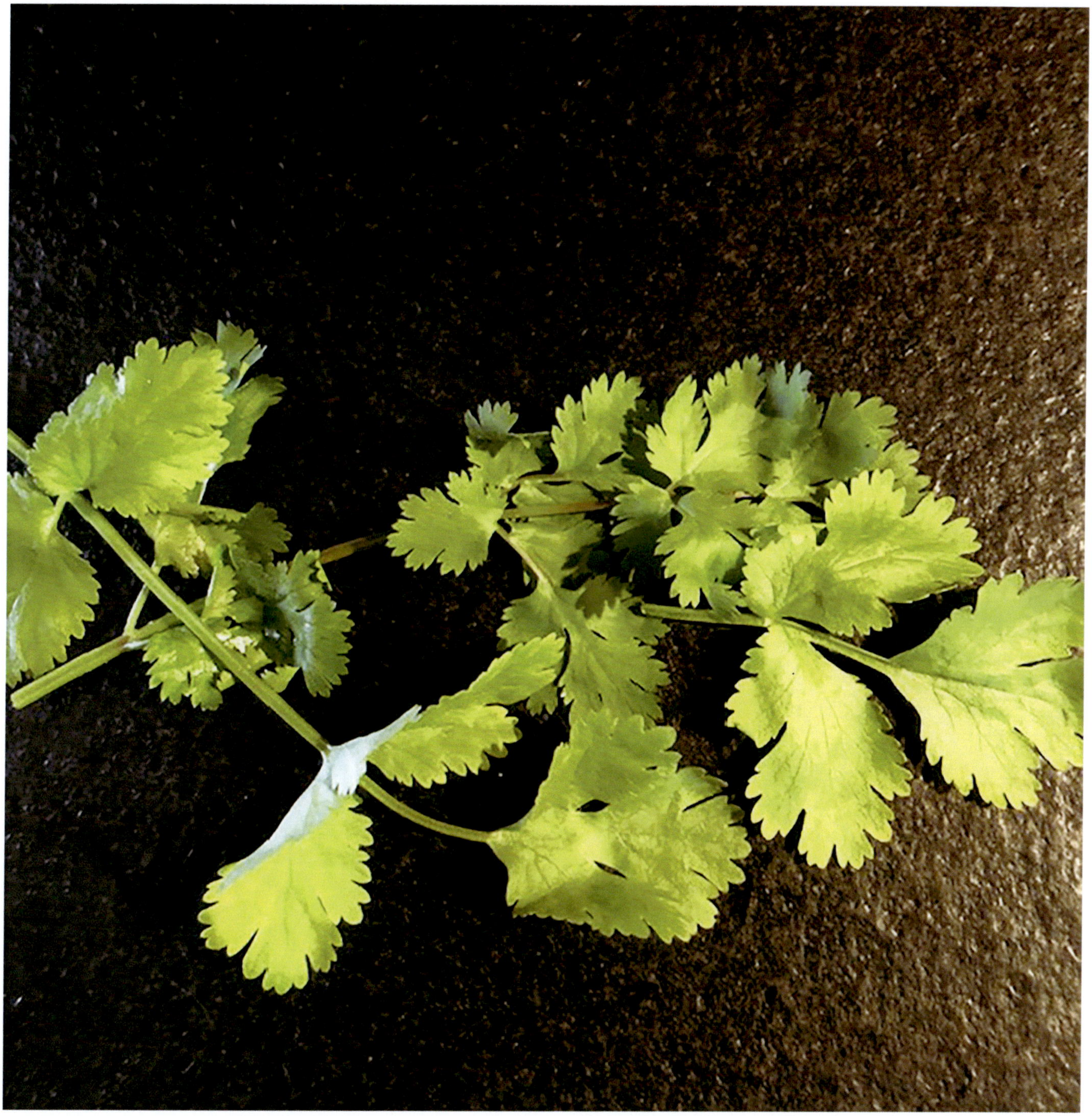

Pepper

Recipe 61

Cacio e Pepe con Tagliolini

Cheese, pepper, and pasta – what else?

Primo Piatto
Serves 2
Cooking time: 25 minutes

Ingredients

250g/9 oz. tagliolini
2tbs butter
1tbs olive oil
Peel of one lemon, thinly sliced 300g/10 oz. pecorino cheese, finely grated, plus more for serving
Cracked peppercorns to taste

Method

In a large saucepan of boiling salted water, cook the pasta until al dente. Drain the pasta in a colander and set aside. But reserve 250ml/1 cup of the pasta water.

Using the same large saucepan, melt the butter and the oil. Add the lemon peel and stir. Then add a generous quantity of cracked black pepper and stir until the mixture becomes fragrant.

Add 125ml/half a cup of the reserved pasta water and mix.

Using tongs, toss in the pasta. Add the cheese and toss again. If the sauce is too thick, add more pasta water and toss.

Serve with more grated cheese and cracked peppercorns.

Pepper

Recipe 62

Salad of Cherry Tomatoes, Fraises Des Bois, Mesclun and Shaved Parmesan Cheese

Fraises des bois are a summer treat and a winner in this salad.

First course
Serves 4
Prep time: 10 minutes
Gluten-free

Ingredients

400g/14 oz. cherry tomatoes, halved
125g/half cup mesclun salad
250g/1 cup fraises des bois
125g half cup parmigiano cheese shavings
Drizzle of extra virgin olive oil and crema di balsamico
A generous amount of freshly ground pepper

Method

On a serving platter, or in 4 individual salad plates, arrange the mesclun leaves, cherry tomatoes, fraise des bois, and shavings of parmigiano cheese.

Drizzle the finest extra virgin olive oil you have and then the crema di balsamico.

Crack a generous amount of freshly ground pepper and serve.

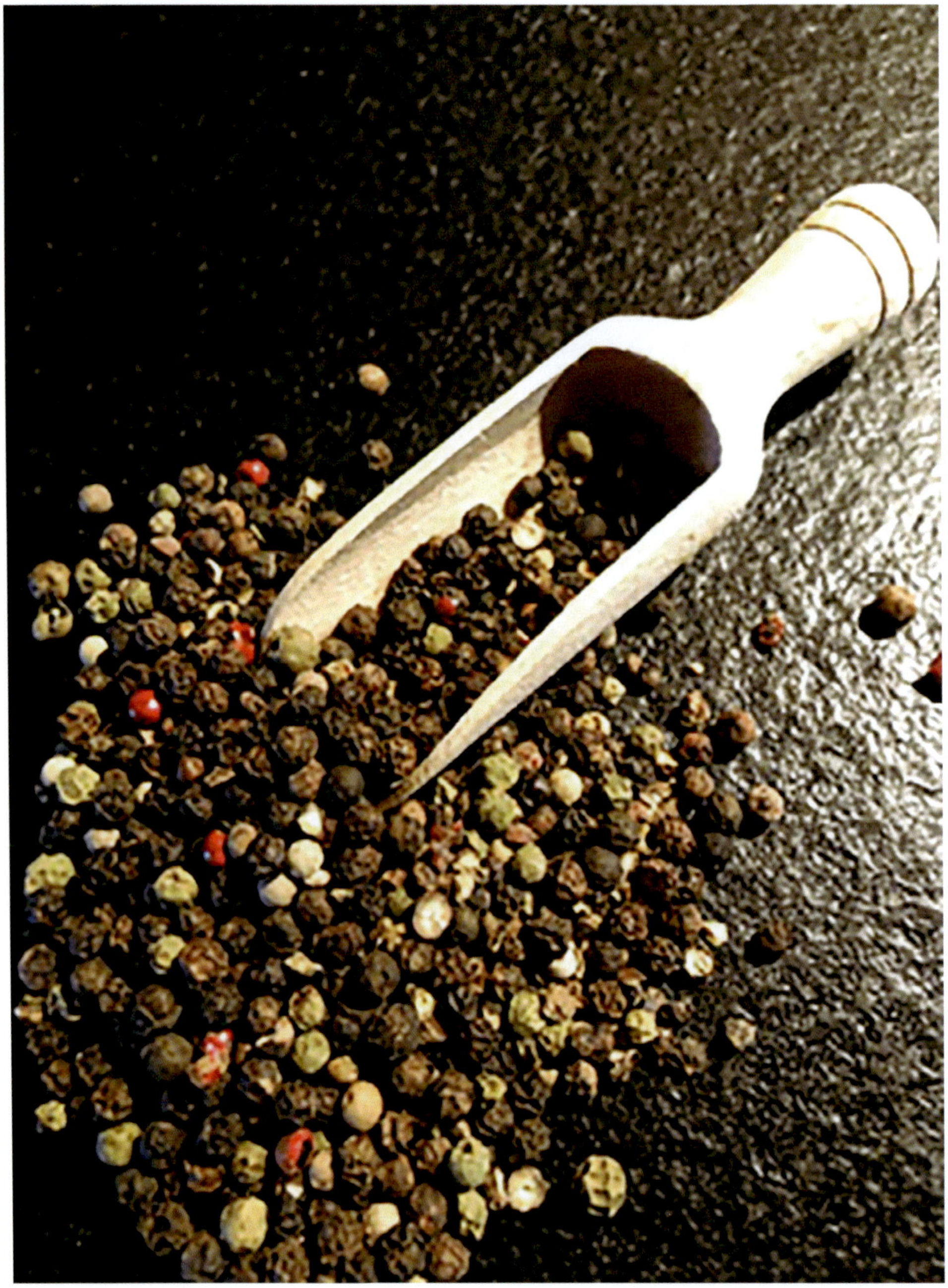

Poppy seeds

Recipe 63

Lemon Poppy-Seed Fairy Cakes

A sunny taste of home

Breakfast or With Afternoon Tea
Makes 12 fairy cakes
Prep time: 15 minutes
Cooking time: 20 minutes

Ingredients

350g/12 oz. white flour
125g/half a cup sugar
2tbs poppy seeds
1tbs baking powder
125g/half a cup melted unsalted butter
125g/half a cup full-fat plain Greek-style yogurt
60ml/quarter cup heavy cream
2 large eggs
Pinch of salt
Zest from one unwaxed lemon
3tbs lemon juice (juice of one large lemon)
Icing sugar/powdered sugar

Method

Preheat oven to 220°C/450°F.

Line your fairy-cake pan with paper wrappers.

Whisk the butter and sugar, adding the eggs, yogurt, heavy cream, lemon juice, baking powder, and salt together to create a batter.

Add flour and poppy seeds to the batter and mix until smooth.

Divide the batter into 10-12 fairy-cake cups, filling each cup 2/3 full and wiping off any batter that may have spilled into the baking pan.

Bake the fairy cakes for 5 minutes at 220°C/450°F. Then reduce the heat to 180°C/350°F and continue baking for another 12 to 15 minutes or until a toothpick inserted in the thickest part of a fairy cake comes out clean or with a few moist crumbs.

Turn the pan upright to cool. Remove the fairy cakes when completely cooled.

Dust with icing/powdered sugar.

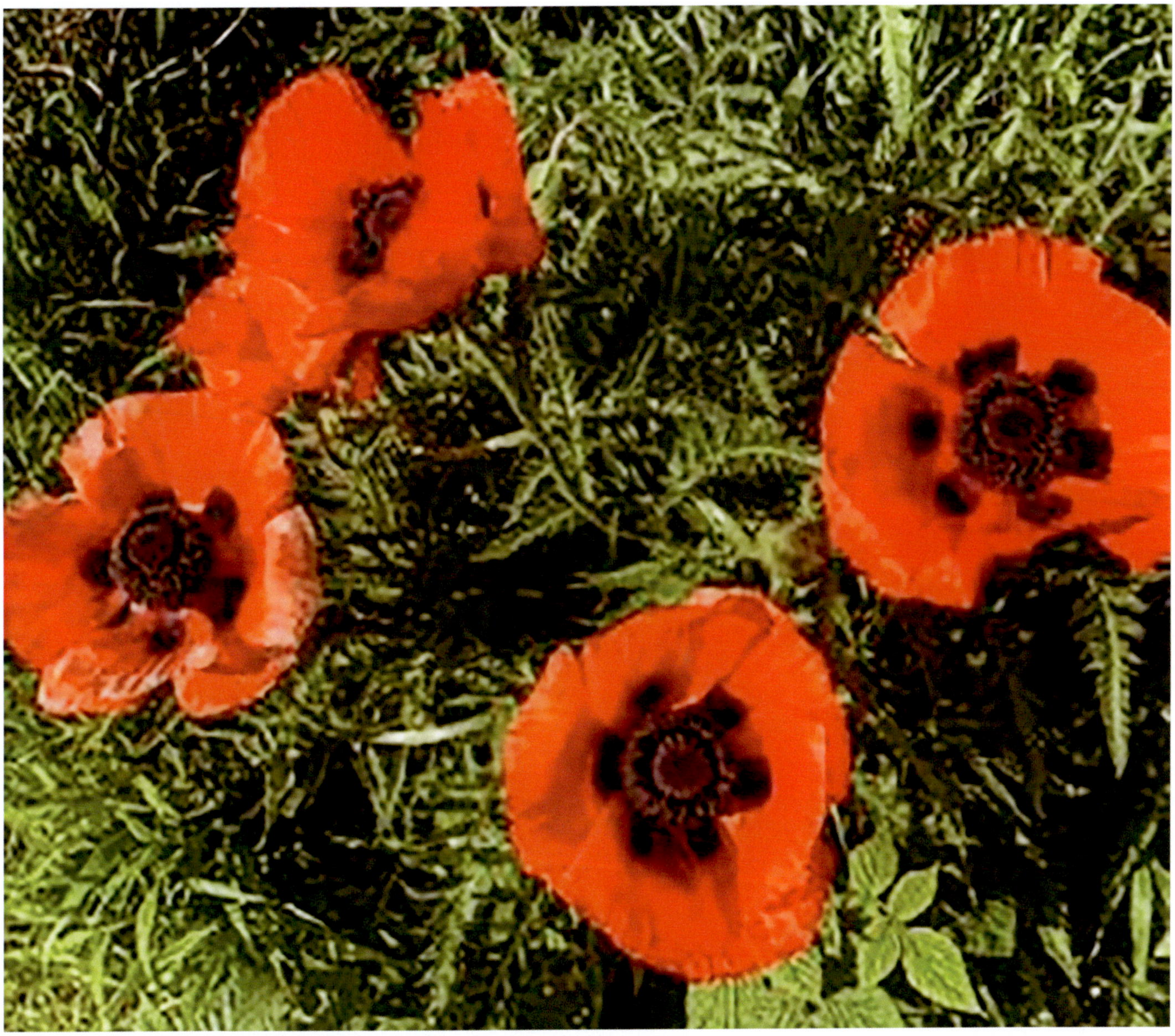

Rose petals

Recipe 64

Duchess of Cambridge Cocktail

Inspired by a recent visit to Rules Restaurant in London and their talented bar staff. Sip the flavours of regal luxury.

Apéro
Serves 2
Prep time: 5 minutes

Ingredients

125ml/8fl oz. pomegranate and rose gin
125ml/8fl oz. elderflower and rose cordial
Juice of 1 lime
A small bunch mint leaves, crushed
Fizz (Champagne or Prosecco), to top up the glasses
Dried rose petals

Method

Fill a cocktail shaker with crushed ice.
Pour in the pomegranate and rose gin, elderflower and rose cordial, lime juice, and crushed mint leaves.
Put the lid on the cocktail shaker and shake until the sides become nice and frosty.
Pour into the prettiest champagne glasses that you own!
Top up the glasses with some fizz.
Garnish with dried rose petals and sip!

Rose petals

Recipe 65

Rose and Pomegranate Ice cream

Pretty in pink and blossoming into delicate scented flavours

Dessert
Serves 4
Cook time: 15 minutes
Chill time: 10 hours
Gluten-free

Ingredients

500ml/1 pint double/heavy cream
1tbs rose water
400ml/14fl oz. condensed milk
2tbs pomegranate molasses
400ml/14fl oz. pomegranate juice
Pomegranate seeds to toss on top
Dried rose petals

Method

Pour the cream, rose water, condensed milk, and pomegranate molasses into a mixing bowl. Use an electric mixer to whisk into soft peaks. Drizzle in the pomegranate juice and whisk by hand until it just becomes thickened. Pour the mixture into a freezer-proof container and freeze for about 2 hours.

Remove from the freezer and whisk thoroughly by hand again. Return the container to the freezer and freeze for another 2 hours. Then whisk again and freeze for a further 5 to 6 hours.

Remove from the freezer 5 minutes before serving and scoop the ice cream into bowls. Sprinkle pomegranate seeds and dried rose petals on top and serve.

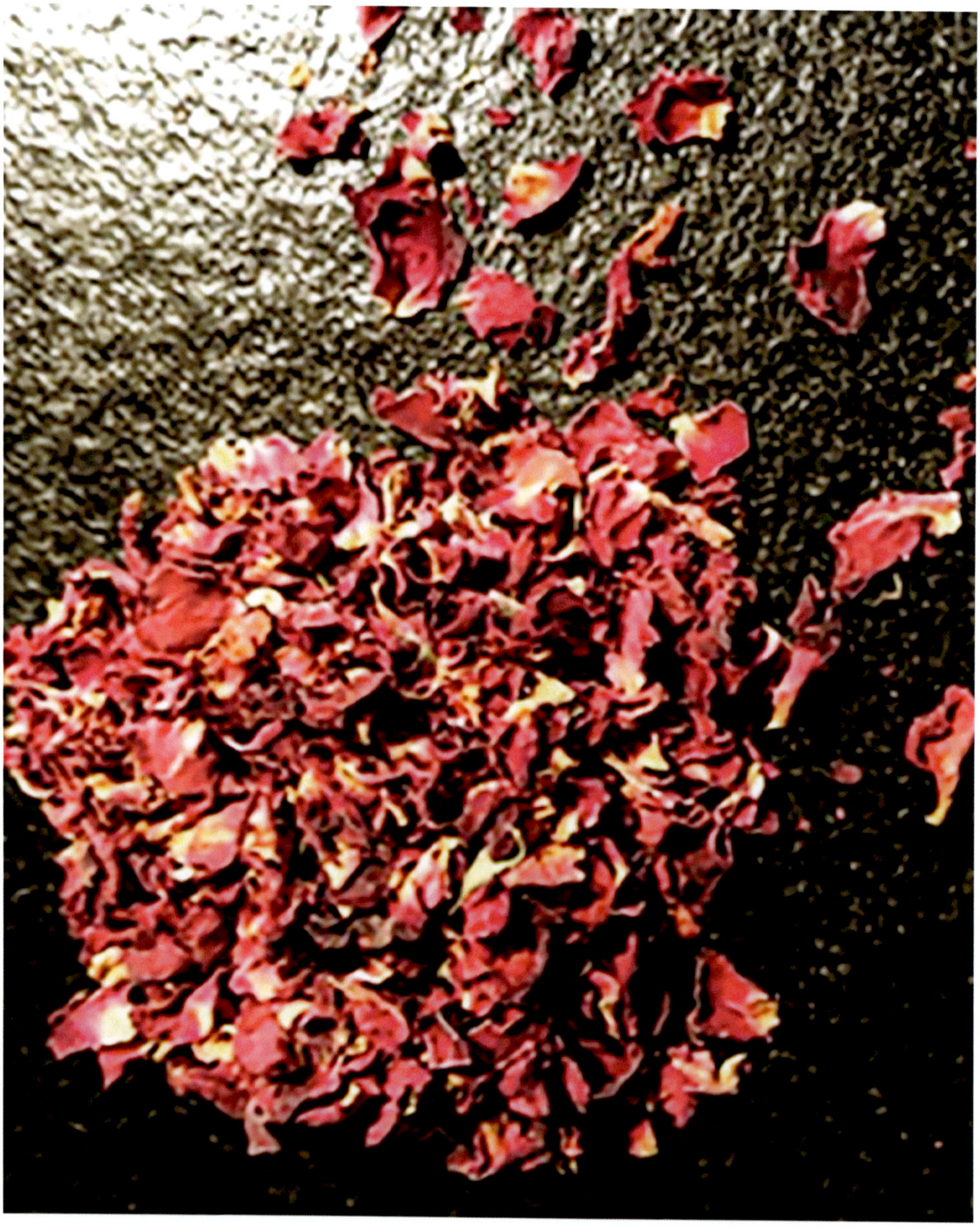

Rosemary

Recipe 66

Rosemary Focaccia

"There's rosemary. That's for remembrance; pray you, love, remember."
William Shakespeare

Bread
Serves 4
Prep time: 3 hours and 30 minutes
Cooking time: 30 minutes

Ingredients

2tbs active dry yeast
375ml/13fl oz. warm water
1 pinch of sugar
950g/2lbs unbleached all-purpose flour, plus some for dusting
1tsp salt
75ml/a third cup extra virgin olive oil, plus some to drizzle
2 pinches coarse ground pepper
1 pinch dried oregano
1 pinch dried sage
1 pinch dried marjoram
1 pinch mild curry powder
Salt flakes to sprinkle
Cracked pepper to sprinkle
3 or 4 sprigs of fresh rosemary
Polenta for baking

Method

Combine the yeast and water in a small bowl, stirring until the yeast is dissolved. Add a pinch of sugar and set aside for 5 minutes.

To create the focaccia dough, sift the flour into a large, warm bowl. Make a hole (a 'well') in the middle of the flour and gently fold in the yeast. Cover with plastic wrap and let it rest in a warm place for 25 minutes.

Turn out the dough on to a lightly dusted floured surface. Knead for 8 to 10 minutes until the dough is smooth and elastic, adding flour (if necessary) to prevent it from becoming too sticky.

Slightly oil the large bowl and place the dough into it. Turn the dough to coat on all sides. Cover with plastic wrap and let rise in a warm place until it doubles in size: 1 to 2 hours.

Punch down the dough on to a lightly dusted floured surface and gently knead in the olive oil, dried herbs, and curry powder.

Line a baking tray with baking paper and sprinkle the polenta on to it. Set aside.

CONTINUED…
Rosemary Focaccia

Roll out the dough on to a lightly dusted floured surface into a rectangle, 4cm/1" thick. Place the rectangle into the baking tray. Cover with a tea towel and let rise until double in size: about 20 to 25 minutes.

Preheat the oven to 220°C/450°F.

Remove the tea towel and press indentations using your index finger into the dough and place a leaf or two of rosemary in each of these indentations.

Sprinkle with salt flakes and cracked pepper. Drizzle a little olive oil.

Place the baking tray into the hot oven and bake for 10 minutes. Then reduce the heat to 180°C/ 350°F and bake another 20 minutes

Remove and transfer to a wire rack to cool.

Rosemary

Recipe 67

Lonza di Maiale Alle Nocciole (Pork Loin with Hazelnut Sauce)

A treat from the Northern Italian region of Piemonte, with hazelnuts and black truffles!

Main course
Serves 6
Prep time: 15 minutes
Cooking time: 50 to 60 minutes

Ingredients

1kg/2lb 4oz pork loin joint
2tbs unsalted butter
2tbs olive oil
2tbs shallots, chopped
3 sprigs of fresh rosemary (plus extra to garnish)
2 bay leaves
250ml/1 cup double/heavy cream
250ml/1 cup rich beef broth
400g/14 oz. hazelnuts, toasted and finely ground
Black truffle shavings: optional
1/2tsp freshly ground white pepper
Pinch of salt

Method

Preheat the oven to 180°C/350°F.

Using your cooktop, in a roasting pan over medium heat, melt the butter and olive oil. Add the shallots, rosemary, and bay leaf and then brown the pork joint on all sides. Add the broth, cream, salt, and pepper, and stir.

Put the roasting pan into the oven and roast until the meat thermometer reads 63°C/145°F (about 45 minutes).

Remove from the oven and place the roast on to a cutting board. Discard the rosemary and bay leaf from the pan and add the hazelnuts to the sauce and stir. With a sharp knife, carve the roast into thick slices. Cover with the sauce and return to the oven to cook for 5 minutes.

To serve

For a true treat from Piemonte, shave black truffle on top. Garnish with fresh rosemary and serve with a full-bodied Barolo wine.

Saffron

Recipe 68

Saffron Chili Butter

A buttery golden sauce. Serve on grilled sea-bass, sautéed scallops, or steamed asparagus.

Sauce
Serves 2
Prep time: 5 minutes
Gluten-free

Ingredients

125g/half a cup unsalted butter, softened
A generous pinch of saffron threads
1 large red chili pepper, seeded and finely chopped
Zest from one lime

Method

Using a fork, mix the saffron threads, red chili, and lime zest into your softened butter.
Add dollops of the saffron butter on top of your fish, seafood, asparagus, or whatever. And serve.

Saffron

Recipe 69

Risotto Milanese with Lemon

An elegant way to start a festive dinner. *Buon appetito!*

Primo Piatto
Serves 4
Cooking time: 45 minutes
Gluten-free
Also see video on my YouTube channel: lockedintastes

                        Risotto alla Milanese with Lemon

Ingredients

750ml/3 cups chicken stock, preferably homemade
250ml/1 cup dry white wine
2tbs extra-virgin olive oil
1 small onion, finely chopped
1 preserved lemon, sliced and chopped
300g/10 oz. Arborio rice
2 pinches of saffron threads
250g/1 cup parmigiano cheese, finely grated
2tbs unsalted butter
Salt and freshly ground pepper to taste

Method

In a medium saucepan, bring the chicken stock to a simmer.

In a large frying pan, heat the olive oil. Add the onion and cook over moderate heat, stirring until softened: about 5 minutes. Now add the rice to the pan and sauté for about 1 minute, stirring constantly, until the rice turns a bright white colour.

Add a third of the warm stock and cook over moderate heat, stirring occasionally, until nearly absorbed. Add the preserved lemon and stir.

Continue to add the stock a third at a time or until the liquid is nearly absorbed.

In a mini mortar and pestle, grind the saffron into a fine powder and then add it to the wine, stirring until the wine colour changes from a pale yellow to a bright orange. Add the wine to the pan and stir occasionally until well absorbed. Stir in the cheese and butter.

The risotto is cooked when the rice is al dente and the sauce thick and creamy: about 40 minutes total. Season with salt and pepper and serve with parmigiano shavings.

Chef's note: If your risotto seems drier than you wish, simply add a bit more of the stock or, preferably, more wine!

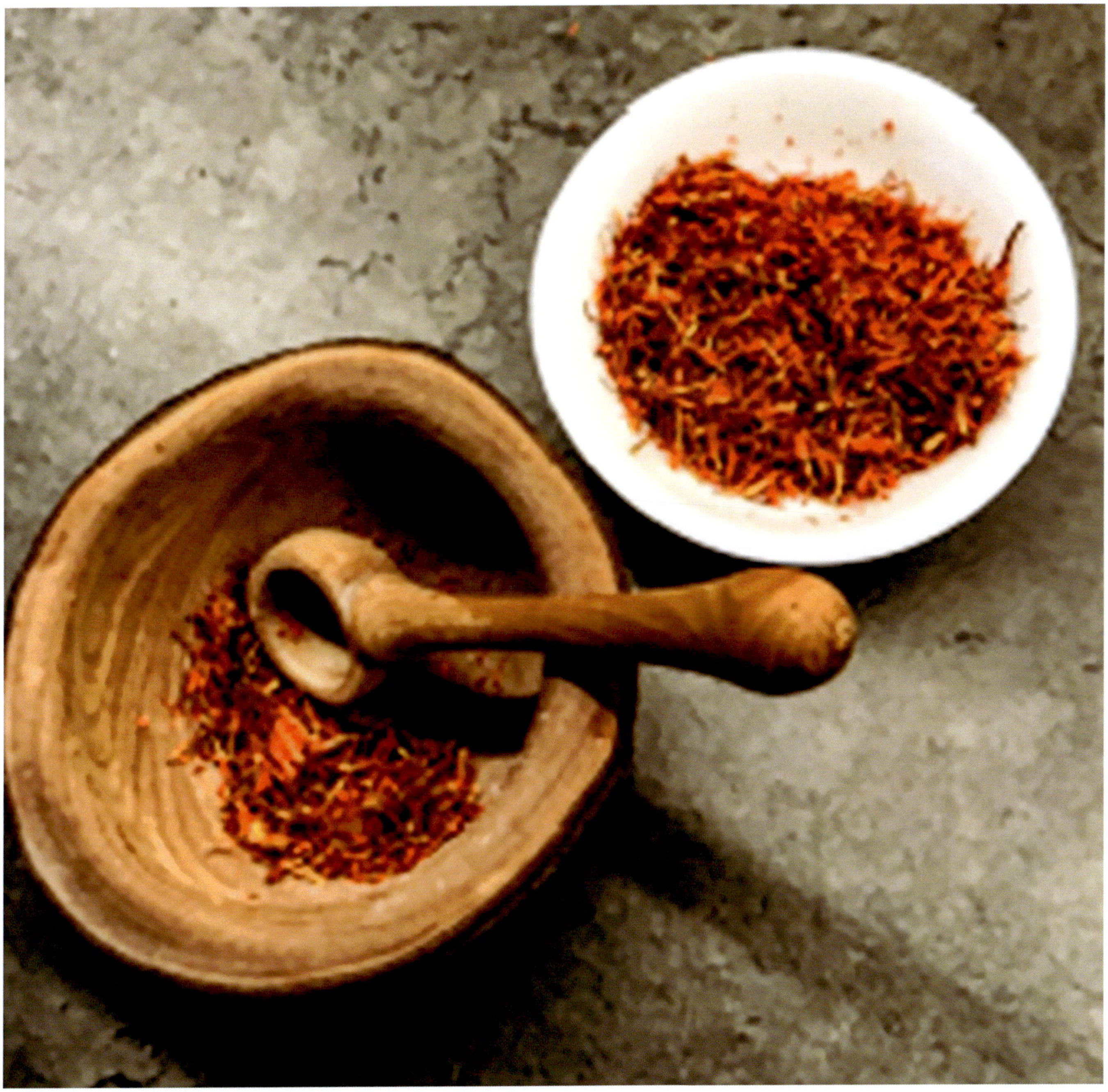

Sage

Recipe 70

Stuffed Zucchini Flowers (Fiori di Zucca)

Enjoy these treats of the first signs of summer. It is pure luxury to munch on these tender and sweet blossoms.

First course
Serves 4
Prep time: 15 minutes
Cook time: 7 to 10 minutes

Also see video on my YouTube channel: lockedintastes

Ingredients

8 zucchini flowers
125g/half cup fine breadcrumbs
125g/half cup ricotta cheese, drained
125g/half cup parmesan cheese, finely grated
150g/5 oz. minced veal or turkey 85g/3 oz. diced pancetta or bacon bits
85g/3 oz. minced parsley
6 sage leaves, finely chopped
Pinch of nutmeg, grated
Flour for dusting
1 egg, beaten
Olive oil

Method

Combine the veal, diced pancetta, breadcrumbs, sage, and parsley into a mini food processor and mix until well blended.

Add the cheeses and nutmeg. Pulse a few times in the food processor to mix thoroughly.

Stuff the flowers with the meat mixture. Roll them into the flour and then into the egg. Then sauté in olive oil until lightly browned.

Once the flowers are brown and crispy, the meat will be cooked: 7 to 10 minutes.

Serve immediately with cracked pepper and slices of lemon

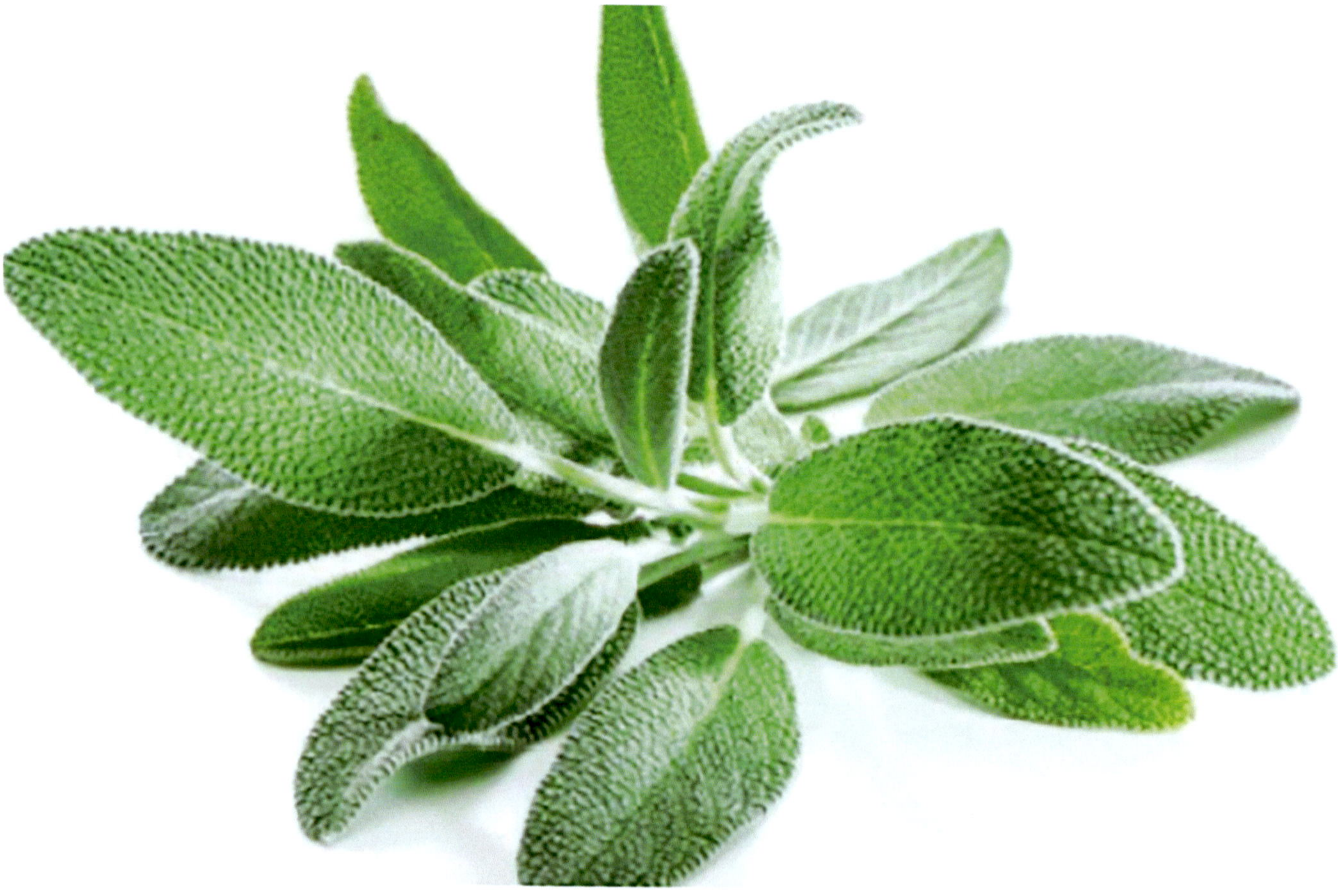

Salt

Recipe 71

Roast Pork with Perfect Crackling

Inspired by Chef James Martin

Main course
Serves: 6
Prep time: 30 minutes plus marinating
Cooking time: 2 hours plus 10 minutes to rest

Ingredients

2tsp freshly ground black pepper
2tsp sea salt
2tbs fennel seeds
60ml/quarter cup olive oil
2kg/4lb 6 oz. rolled and tied pork loin with skin scored (or ask your butcher to prepare)
1 large bulb of fresh fennel, thinly sliced
2 leeks, thinly sliced
2 lemons, sliced

For the gravy

2tsp corn flour
250ml/1 cup Marsala wine
250ml/1 cup hot vegetable or chicken stock

Method

Place the pork, skin side up, in your very clean kitchen sink. Pour over a kettle of boiling water to tighten the skin, which will turn white. Let rest for 5 minutes.
Pat dry with kitchen towels and place on a chopping board.
Rub the olive oil, salt, and pepper all over the roast.
In your baking pan, layer the lemon slices first, then the fennel, and finally

the leeks. Place your seasoned pork on top.

Leave to rest for 1 hour.

Preheat the oven to 230°C/450°F.

Drizzle a little more olive oil and sprinkle the fennel seeds on the top of the pork.

Roast for 30 minutes at 230°C/450°F. Then turn the heat down to 180°C/350°F and continue to roast for 1 hour and 15 minutes.

Remove the pork and let rest for 30 minutes. Your crackling should be very crisp. If not, place the roast under the grill for 5 minutes or so.

While the roast is resting, it's time to make your gravy.

Pour the contents of the roasting pan through a sieve into medium saucepan. Discard the solids, leaving the stock in the saucepan. Skim off the layer of fat.

Put the corn flour into a mug and add a quarter cup of the stock. Stir rapidly to eliminate lumps. Then add back to the hot stock in the saucepan to make gravy.

Pour in the Marsala and let it bubble and then simmer gently for about 10 minutes. Adjust seasoning if needed.

Carve and serve, with loads of healthy green vegetables, roasted potatoes, and the gravy.

Salt

Recipe 72

A grand presentation which creates a super moist fish dish

Main course
Serves 4
Cooking time: 30 minutes
Resting time: 10 minutes
Gluten-free
Dairy-free

Ingredients

2 whole sea bass, cleaned, about 1kg/2lbs each
4 lemons, sliced
6 bay leaves
A bunch of fennel tops
2 to 3kg/5-6lbs coarse salt
A drizzle of lemon-infused olive oil

Method

Preheat oven to 200ºC/400ºF.
Wash and dry the fish. Stuff the cavity with the herbs and lemons and place it on a generous bed of salt in your roasting pan. Cover the whole fish with the remaining salt. Drizzle a little water and with your hands compress the salt on to the fish.
Place the fish in the preheated oven and bake for 30 minutes.
Remove the fish and allow it to rest for about 10 minutes. Note: the fish will continue to cook during the resting time.
To serve
Crack the salt and pull it away from the fish. The skin should pull away with the salt crust.
Gently de-bone the fish as you place the pieces on to your serving platter. Drizzle with lemon-infused olive oil. Serve with new potatoes, fennel and orange salad, and lots fresh lemon.

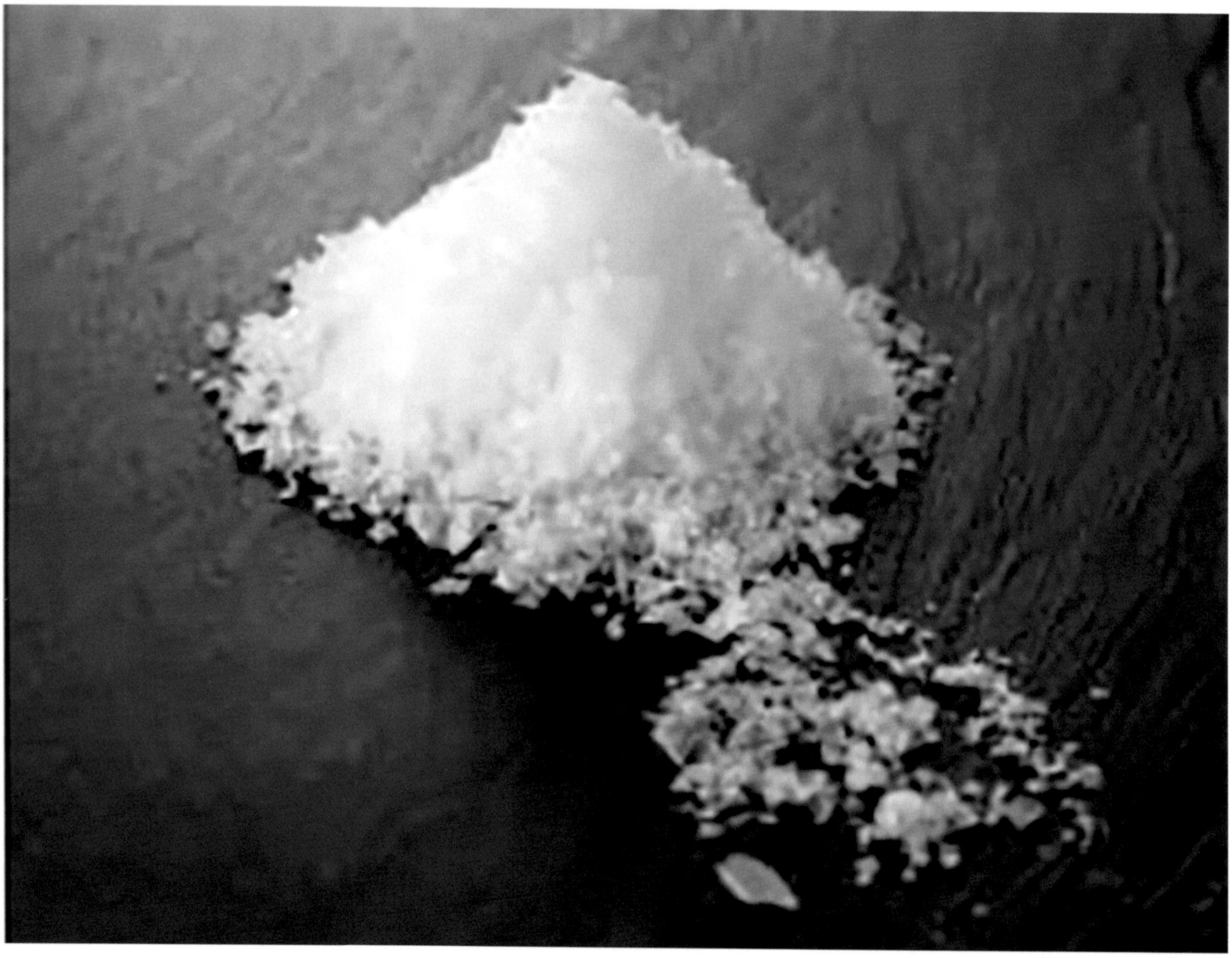

Sesame seeds

Recipe 73

Chinese Lemon Chicken

Also fabulous with prawns or thick white fish such as cod or tofu!

Main Course
Serves: 2
Cook Time: 20 minutes
Gluten-free

Ingredients

2 chicken breasts, cut into cubes
2 egg whites
50g/2 oz. corn flour
1/2tsp salt
2tsp sherry or rice vinegar
1/4tsp baking powder
1/8tsp baking soda

For the sauce

1tbs fresh ginger, minced
375ml/13 oz. strong chicken broth
2tbs fresh lemon juice
1tbs lemon zest
1/2tbs soy sauce
75ml/fresh lemon juice
60ml/2fl oz. rice vinegar
250g/1 cup granulated sugar
2 red chilies, sliced and seeded or 1/4tsp red pepper flakes
3tbs corn flour
2tbs water
1/2tsp sesame oil
Secret ingredient: splash of Limoncello

To serve

Sesame seeds
Fresh lemon slices

Method

Combine the egg whites, corn flour, salt, sherry, baking powder, and baking soda in a medium bowl and stir. Pour over chicken in a re-sealable plastic bag and refrigerate for at least 30 minutes. Remove the chicken pieces from the bag, shake off the excess liquid, and give them another roll in corn flour (to create a thicker coating).

To make the sauce, in a bowl, stir together all sauce ingredients, except for the ginger, green onion, and lemon slices. Set aside.

Pour vegetable oil into a hot wok or a heavy skillet and carefully drop the chicken into the oil. Fry until crispy golden-brown on all sides. Using tongs, transfer the chicken pieces to kitchen paper to absorb the excess oil.

Rinse out the wok/skillet. Add a teaspoon or so of oil. Sauté the ginger for 30 seconds and then add the sauce. Bring the sauce to the boil. Reduce heat to low. Simmer for 10 minutes, stirring occasionally.

Return the cooked chicken pieces to the wok/skillet and add green onions.

Stir to coat and bring the sauce to a low simmer. Add the splash of limoncello and cook for 5 minutes.

Garnish with sesame seeds and serve with steamed rice and fresh lemon.

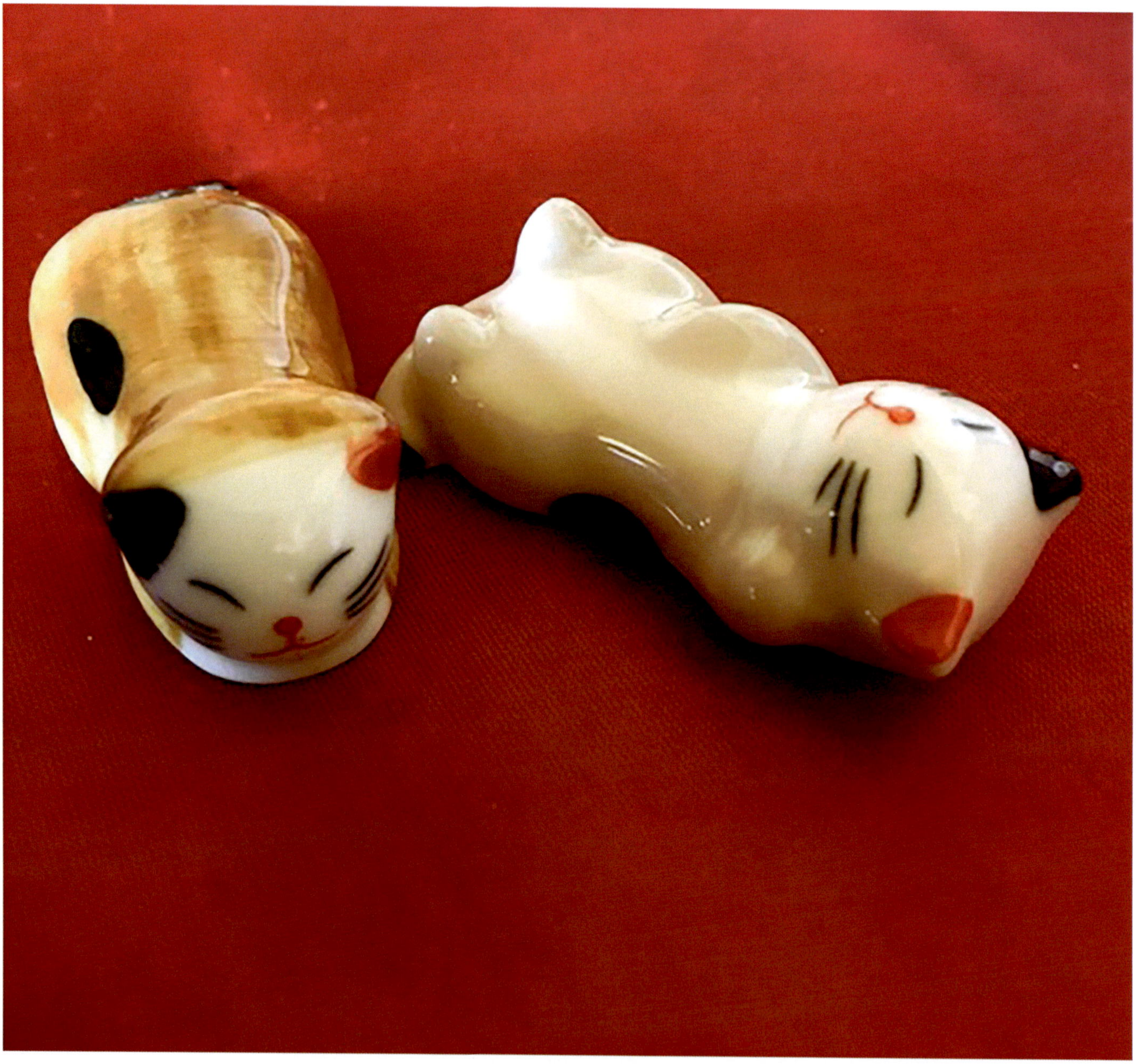

Sesame seeds

Recipe 74

Teriyaki Salmon

Recipe inspired by Chef Chris Bavin. I believe you will find it's a winner.

Main course
Serves 4
Cooking time: 15 minutes
plus marination time
Gluten-free

Ingredients

8cm/3" piece of fresh ginger, peeled and grated
4tbs soy sauce, gluten-free
2tbs sweet chili sauce
1tsp sesame oil
Zest and juice of 1 lime
4 x 150g/5-6 oz. salmon fillets
1tbs vegetable oil

To serve

Pak choi or tenderstem broccoli
1tbs sesame seeds
1 chili pepper, deseeded and sliced, to taste
Small handful of coriander
Slices of lime
Steamed rice

Method

In a dish that is large enough to fit the salmon, mix together the ginger, soy sauce, chili sauce, sesame oil, and the zest and juice of the lime. Place the salmon fillets in the sauce and turn them over to cover them completely.
Marinate in the fridge for 8 or up to 24 hours.
Heat the oil in a frying pan over medium heat. Remove the salmon from the

marinade, letting any excess sauce drip off. Put the sauce to one side.

Place the salmon in the pan, skin-side down. Cook the salmon for 3 minutes. Then pour the reserved marinade over the salmon and turn it over to cook for another 5 to 6 minutes. If the sauce becomes too thick and sticky, simply add a tablespoon of white wine.

Place on to a serving platter. Sprinkle the sesame seeds, chili, coriander, and slices of lime. Serve with steamed rice and pak choi or broccoli.

Star anise

Recipe 75

Spicy Grilled Beef Filet

The star anise provides a unique and welcome zing to this dish.

Main Course
Serves 4
Prep Time: 15 minutes
Marinating time: 2 hours
Cooking time: 8 to 15 minutes
Gluten-free

Ingredients

450g/1lb beef filet
Versatile spicy Thai savoury sauce (See Recipe 36.)
25g/1 oz. star anise
1tps roasted cumin seeds
2tps Szechuan pepper
Red and green chilies, seeded and sliced, to garnish
Coriander leaves, to garnish

Method

In a jar, first prepare a portion of the versatile spicy Thai savoury sauce (Recipe 36).

Then put the roasted cumin seeds and Szechuan pepper into a grinder or pestle and mortar and grind until fine. Then add these ground spices plus star anise to the jar of versatile spicy Thai savoury sauce. Shake it to make a spicy marinade.

Trim the filet, removing all sinew, and slice it into four portions. Put these into a re-sealable plastic bag and pour in the spicy marinade. Allow the beef to marinate for 2 hours.

Heat your grill or grill pan (if cooking on your hob). Shake the excess marinade off the beef and place the beef on to the grill. Cook until rare-medium or well-done, as preferred.

Garnish with torn coriander leaves and sliced green and red chili peppers and serve.

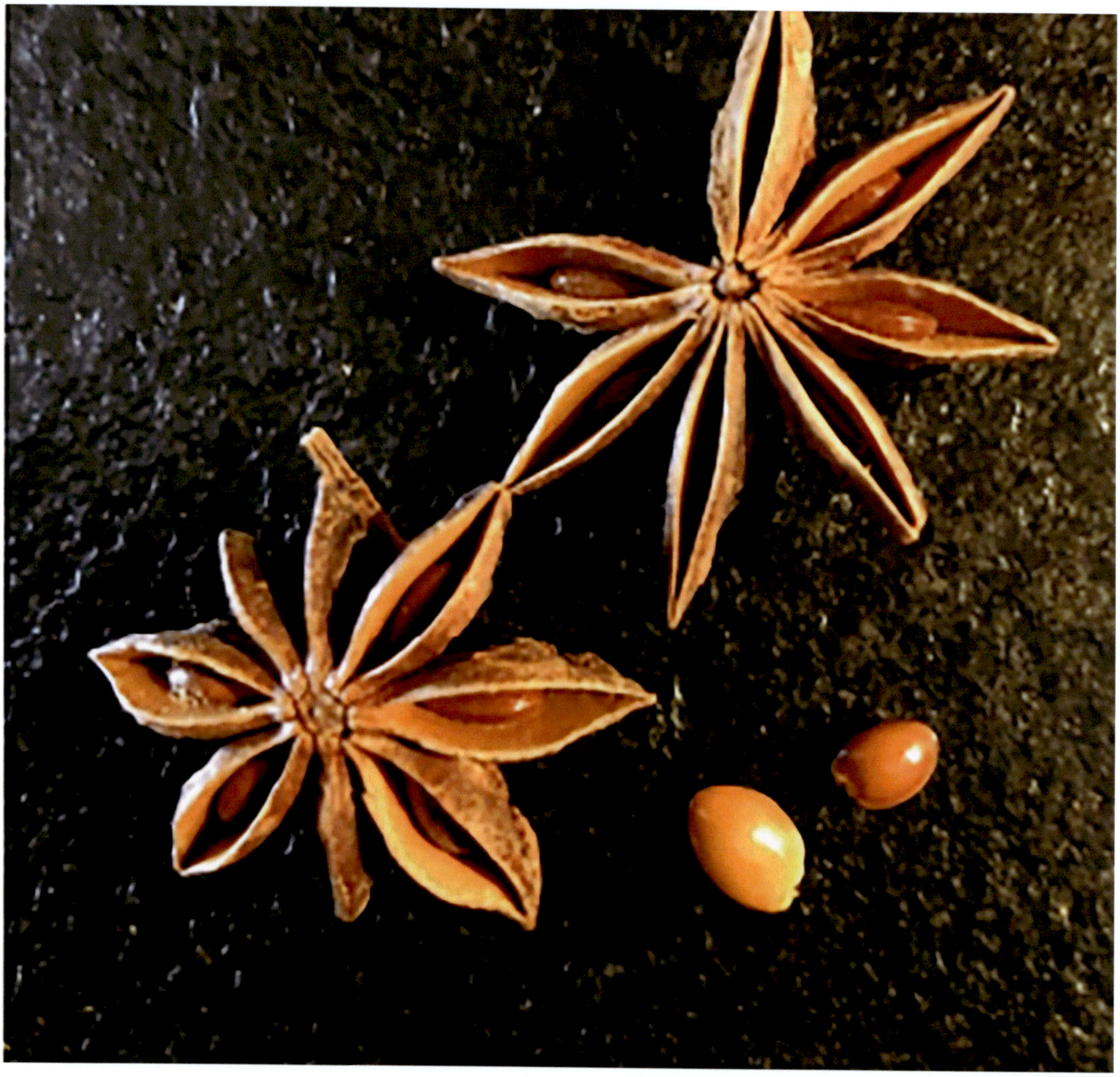

Sumac

Recipe 76

Grilled Mediterranean Vegetables with Lemon-Infused Olive Oil

A healthy side dish filled with the flavours from the Middle East

Side dish
Serves 4
Prep time: 30 minutes
Cooking time: 30 minutes
Gluten-free

Ingredients

1 medium aubergine
1 medium courgette
1 red pepper
1 yellow pepper
60ml/2fl oz. extra-virgin olive oil
Drizzle of lemon-infused olive oil
1tsp salt
2tbs crushed sumac
Fresh sprigs of oregano, for garnish

Method

Cut the aubergine and courgette into 1cm slices and place into a large bowl.

Cut the peppers in half and remove the seeds and white membranes. Then halve the halves and place into the bowl with the aubergine.

Drizzle the olive oil and sprinkle the salt and sumac over the vegetables. Toss and leave to rest for 10 minutes.

Preheat the grill to 220ºC/425ºF. Put the aubergines on the grill first and then the peppers, followed by the courgettes.

Cook the aubergines, peppers, and courgettes on one side for 6 minutes and then flip and cook for an additional 4 to 5 minutes. (Keep an eye on the courgettes, as they may cook faster than the aubergines and peppers.) Remove from grill and place on a serving platter.

To serve

Drizzle with lemon-infused olive oil and garnish with sprigs of oregano.

Sumac

Recipe 77

Salad Olivieh

This dish of Russian origin was created by Chef Lucien Olivieh for the Hermitage in 1860. It is popular not only in Russia but throughout Eastern Europe and is now also a staple in London after most Iranian restaurants.

Side dish or starter
Serves 4
Prep time: 60 minutes
Chilling time: 60 minutes
Gluten-free

Ingredients

1 whole chicken breast, steamed or boiled and shredded
5 medium potatoes, peeled, boiled, and in chunks
2 eggs, hard boiled and chopped
125g/half a cup peas, cooked
250g/1 cup mayonnaise
250g/1 cup natural Greek-style yogurt
Juice of 1 lime
Salt and pepper to taste
1tbs sumac
Lettuce leaves

Method

The chicken, potatoes, eggs, and peas are best precooked and then chilled in order to assemble the salad quickly.
In a bowl, mix together the mayonnaise, yogurt, and lime juice.
Add the shredded chicken and stir.
Mix in the potatoes, peas, and eggs.
Chill for 1 hour.
Place the salad on a bed of crispy lettuce. Sprinkle the sumac over the dish and serve.

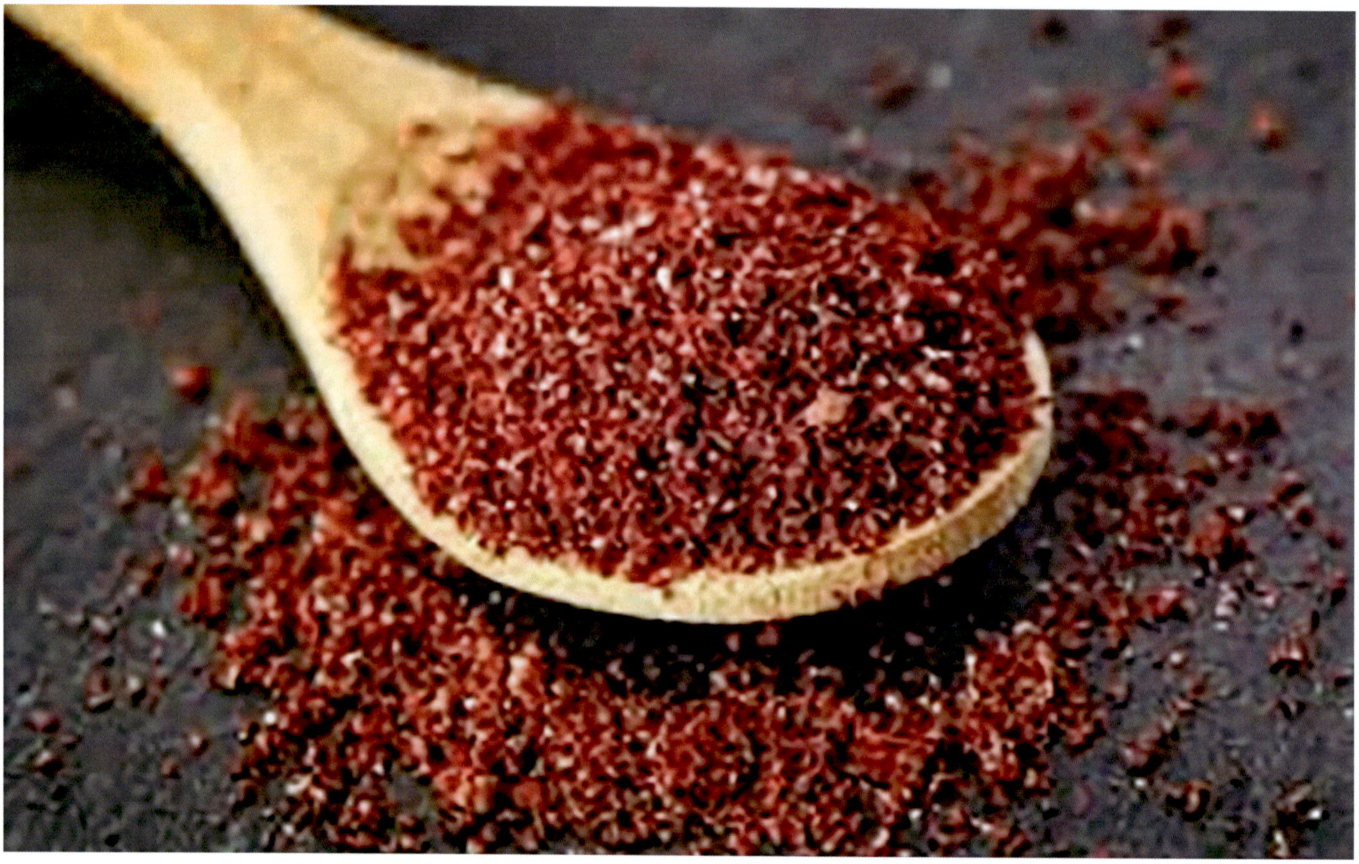

Tamarind

Recipe 78

Roast Quail with Tamarind and Orange Glaze

A flavourful Asian twist on a classic British dish

Main course
Serves 2
Prep time: 10 minutes
Cooking time: 25 minutes
Gluten-free

Roast Quail with Tamarind and Orange Glaze

Ingredients

4 quails
4tbs of tamarind paste
250ml/1 cup freshly squeezed orange juice
Juice of one lime
1 whole orange, sliced
1tbs ginger paste
2 large red chilies, seeded and chopped
4tsp garam masala
120ml/4fl oz. honey
4tbs butter
120ml/4fl oz. cream sherry
Chopped coriander
Salt to taste

Method

Place the tamarind, orange juice, lime juice, ginger, garam masala, chilies, honey, butter, and sherry into a saucepan and simmer for 5 to 7 minutes to reduce. Add salt to taste.

Preheat the oven to 220°C/425°F.

Rinse the quails and place them into a baking dish, breast side up.

Pour half of the tamarind sauce on the quails and place sliced oranges around them. Keep the rest of the sauce on a low simmer to reduce.

Roast for 20 to 25 minutes. The quails should be golden and the juices clear.

Place the quails on to a serving dish and spoon over the rest of the now-reduced tamarind sauce. Garnish with coriander. Now serve!

Variation: try a whole salmon filet instead of quails.

DRY TAMARIND

Tamarind à sec • Vertrocknet Tamarinde
Secco Tamarindo • Seco Tamarindo • Torka Tamarind
Kuivattu Tamarind • تمر هندي • इमली

# Thai basil

Recipe 79

Pad Krapao

Thai basil with mince of your choice: pork, chicken, turkey, or plant-base

Main course
Serves 3 to 4
30 to 35 minutes
Gluten-free

Also see video on my YouTube channel: lockedintastes

Ingredients

3 tablespoons vegetable oil
2 shallots, thinly sliced
2 stalks lemon grass, thinly sliced
8cm/3" piece of ginger, minced
3 red Thai chili peppers, deseeded and thinly sliced
500g/2 cups mince (of your choice)
1tsp sugar
1tbs fish sauce
2tbs dark soy sauce
2tsp oyster sauce
2 limes, squeezed
250ml/1 cup chicken broth or white wine
3 kaffir lime leaves, cut into matchsticks with scissors
1 large bunch of Thai basil (Do not substitute with Italian basil.)
1 medium cucumber, sliced
2 more red chili peppers sliced to add as a garnish

Method

To make the chili paste:
In a mortar and pestle, first pound the chopped ginger and then continue to pound while adding the shallots, lemongrass, and red chili peppers until it all becomes a well-incorporated thick paste. Set aside.
In a wok, over medium-high heat, add the oil, then the chili paste, and fry for 2 to 3 minutes.

Crank up the heat to high and add the mince, breaking it up into small bits and allowing it to crisp up. Add the fish sauce, dark soy sauce, oyster sauce, lime juice, and sugar.

Stir-fry for another minute and add the wine or broth. Because your pan is over high heat, the liquid should cook off very quickly while adding tons of flavour. Add the kaffir lime leaves and the Thai basil and stir-fry until the basil wilts.

Garnish with sliced cucumbers and red chili peppers and serve with steamed jasmine rice.

Thai basil

Recipe 80

Thai Red Curry with Duck Breasts (Gaeng Pet Ped Yang)

Totally addictive and authentic tastes of Thailand in every bite

Main course
Serves 4
Prep time: 10 minutes
Cooking time: 30 minutes

Ingredients

2 duck breasts, skin removed, sliced into strips
150g/5 oz. red curry paste (ingredients below)
250ml (1 cup) coconut milk
125ml/half cup chicken stock
1 courgette, halved and sliced into thick pieces
2 tomatoes, cubed
6 baby corn, halved
A bunch of fresh Thai basil leaves
Coconut cream, to drizzle

For the red curry paste

125g/half cup ginger, minced
4 red chili peppers, seeded
2 shallots
Juice from 2 limes
1tbs sugar
2tbs fish sauce or light soy sauce
Pinch of salt
2 stalks of lemongrass, chopped

Method

To make the paste

In a mini food processor, place the ginger, shallots, lemon grass, chili peppers, lime juice, fish sauce, sugar and salt. Pulse until it forms a thick paste about 5 to 7 minutes.

In a medium-sized saucepan, bring the stock and coconut milk to the boil. Then spoon in the red chili paste and simmer for 10 minutes.

To prepare the dish

Add the duck and continue to simmer for 25 minutes. (It's a good moment to steam or boil your jasmine rice.)

Add your vegetables to the saucepan and simmer for another 5 minutes.

Add the Thai basil to the saucepan 10 seconds before you are about to serve.

Spoon curry into a serving bowl or on to individual plates. Drizzle the coconut cream.

Serve with steamed jasmine rice.

Variation: try beef or salmon instead of duck.

Thyme

Recipe 81

Polenta with Roasted Mushrooms and Thyme

Mountain cuisine at its best – hearty, rustic, and full of flavour

Main course
Serves 4
Prep time: 15 minutes
Cooking time: 30 minutes

Ingredients

1 liter/4 cups chicken broth
500g/2 cups polenta
2tbs olive oil, plus a drizzle
500g/1lb mixed exotic mushrooms, such as porcini, cremini, oyster, maitake, shiitake, or chanterelles
2tbs of butter or goose fat
250g/1 cup grated pecorino, grana padano, or parmigiano
A bunch of fresh thyme
Truffle oil, to drizzle
Salt and pepper

Method

Bring the chicken broth to a rapid boil. Slowly pour in the polenta, whisking aggressively to eliminate lumps. Take care, as the polenta may bubble and spit.

Reduce the heat and continue whisking gently for about 5 minutes. The polenta will start to thicken. Then cover and simmer for a further 30 minutes.

While the polenta is simmering, rinse the mushrooms to remove any grit and dry them in a salad spinner. Slice and set aside.

Preheat the oven to 220°C/425°F.

Melt the butter or goose fat in a baking tray under the oven grill for 30 seconds. Remove quickly before it starts to burn.

Place the mushrooms in the baking tray. Sprinkle in salt and cracked pepper and add 8 sprigs of fresh thyme. Stir so that the mushrooms are well coated.

Place the tray under the grill for 7 to 10 minutes. Remove from grill and serve.
   Divide the polenta into serving bowls. Spoon the mushrooms on top and sprinkle generous amounts of grated cheese. Drizzle with truffle oil. Garnish with fresh sprigs of thyme and serve.

Thyme

Recipe 82

Stuffed Peppers in a Mascarpone Tomato Sauce

A warming meal to enjoy on a chilly night

Main course
Serves 4
Prep time: 30 minutes
Cooking time: 40 minutes
Gluten-free

Ingredients
For the stuffed peppers

4 large red peppers, seeded and sliced in half
125g/half a cup cooked basmati rice
2 chopped shallots
85g/3 oz. chopped fennel
1 egg, beaten
Splash of olive oil
250g/1 cup minced lamb or, or use a meat substitute
150g/5 oz. crumbled feta cheese plus 100g/4 oz. for serving
A large handful of fresh thyme leaves, stems removed
Salt and pepper
2tbs olive oil
For the mascarpone sauce
400g/14 oz. tinned crushed tomatoes
Splash of olive oil
Pinch of sugar
125ml/half cup vegetable stock
60ml/quarter cup red or white wine
120g/half cup mascarpone cheese
Drizzle of crema di balsamico
Salt and pepper

Method
The stuffed peppers

In a sauté pan, drizzle the olive oil and heat over high heat. Add the chopped shallots and fennel and cook for 5 minutes or until they are soft. Place in a large mixing bowl.

Now add to the mixing bowl the cooked rice, minced lamb, thyme, feta cheese, egg, salt, and pepper and mix until the ingredients are well combined.

Stuff the peppers with the mixture and place into a roasting pan. Set aside while you make the sauce.

The mascarpone sauce

In a medium-sized saucepan over high heat, drizzle the olive oil and add the tomatoes. Stir and cook for 3 minutes.

Lower the heat to medium and add the stock, wine, pinch of sugar, salt, and pepper and stir occasionally for 5 to 7 minutes.

Now whisk in the mascarpone cheese and cook for another 5 minutes.

Add the drizzle of crema di balsamico and continue to simmer for 5 minutes more.

Putting it together

Pour the sauce over the stuffed peppers, cover with a lid or aluminium foil, and bake for 35 minutes. Then remove the cover, sprinkle the remaining feta cheese, and bake for an additional 5 to 7 minutes.

Serve with crusty bread.

Tumeric

Recipe 83

Grilled Aubergine with Turmeric, Chili Peppers and Pomegranate Seeds

Exotic South Asian tastes from the grill to your table

Starter or side dish
Serves 4
Cook time: 20 minutes
Gluten-free

Ingredients

4 small aubergines, sliced lengthwise
125ml/half a cup olive oil, plus a little more for brushing
1tbs ground turmeric
Juice of one lime
1 pinch of salt
1 pinch of sugar
A handful of pomegranate seeds
3 chopped green chili peppers

Method

Slice the aubergines lengthwise and brush liberally with olive oil. Then sprinkle the turmeric, together with the pinches of salt and sugar, over the aubergines and toss. The flesh of the aubergines will turn a brilliant yellow.

Fire up your grill. When very hot, place the aubergines on the grill and cook for 6 minutes. Then flip and cook the other side for 4 minutes, checking to make sure that they are not burning!

Remove and place on to a serving platter. Drizzle some olive oil, the pomegranate seeds, and the chopped chili peppers. Serve with grilled flatbread and Greek-style yogurt.

Vanilla bean

Recipe 84

Vanilla Crème Brûlée

A satisfying vanilla-infused, creamy, and crunchy ending to a meal

Dessert
Serves 6
Prep time: 15 minutes
Cooking time: 35 minutes
Chilling time: 4 to 5 hours
Gluten-free

Vanilla Crème Brûlée

Ingredients
6 large egg yolks
120g/half a cup caster sugar
1 vanilla bean
60g/quarter cup turbinado sugar (light brown raw sugar)
500ml/1 pint double/heavy cream
Also needed
6 ramekins
Kitchen blowtorch

Method

Preheat the oven 160°C/325°F.

Pour the cream into a medium-sized saucepan and allow to simmer over low heat.

Slice the vanilla bean down the middle. Scrape the seeds into the cream and then drop in the pod as well. (The pod adds more flavour.)

In a mixing bowl, beat the yolks and pour in the sugar in a stream. Beat until pale yellow and frothy.

Gradually add the warmed cream into this egg and sugar mixture, constantly whisking with a wire whisk to make a custard. Remove the pod and any skin that may have formed.

Pour the mixture into individual ramekins. Place them into a roasting pan, surrounded by hot water, two-thirds of the way up. Cook in the oven until set: 30 to 35 minutes. (The custard will be a bit jiggly-wiggly in the centre.)

Remove ramekins from oven. Allow to cool. Then place in the refrigerator to chill for 4 to 5 hours.

Before serving, sprinkle the raw sugar on to each ramekin. Then caramelise the sugar with the blowtorch. If you like your topping to be extra crunchy and thick, repeat this step to make a second layer!

Serve immediately.

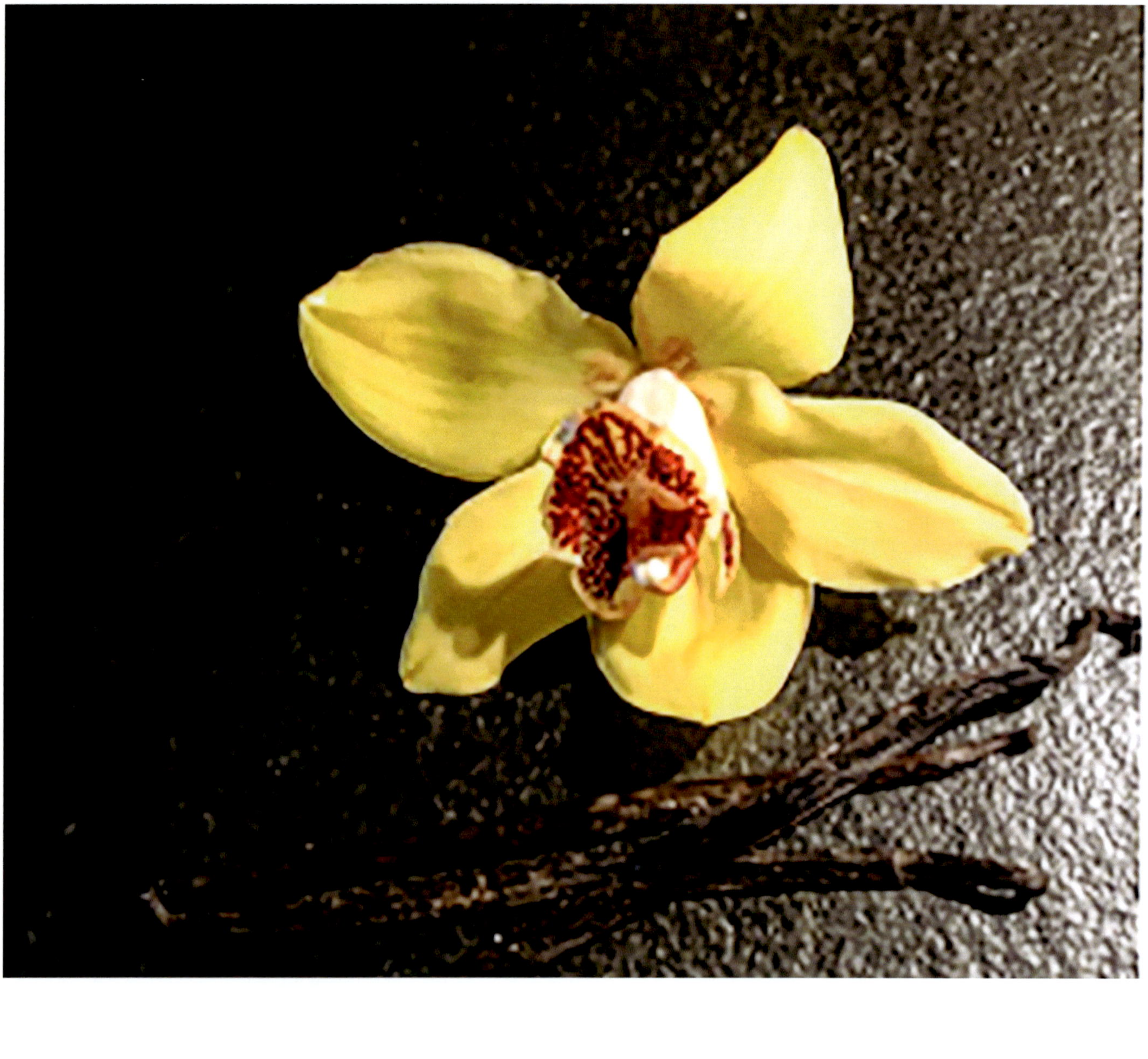

Vanilla bean

Recipe 85

Sautéed Green Beans with Vanilla-Salt and Butter

Flavoured salts are innovative and allow us to blend tastes delicately rather than overpowering our palate.

Side dish
Serves 4
Prep time: 5 minutes
Cooking time: 15 minutes
Gluten-free

Ingredients

500g/2 cups fine green beans, trimmed
3tbs of unsalted butter
1tsp vanilla salt
Pinch of sugar

Method

In a large sauté pan, bring 125ml/half a cup of water to the boil. Add the green beans and cook for 10 minutes.

Drain the beans and place them back into the hot pan so that the excess water evaporates (approx. 1 minute). Place into a serving dish.

In a small saucepan, melt the butter on medium heat, taking care that it does not burn. Add the pinch of sugar and the vanilla salt and cook for 1 minute.

Pour the vanilla-salted butter over the hot beans and serve.

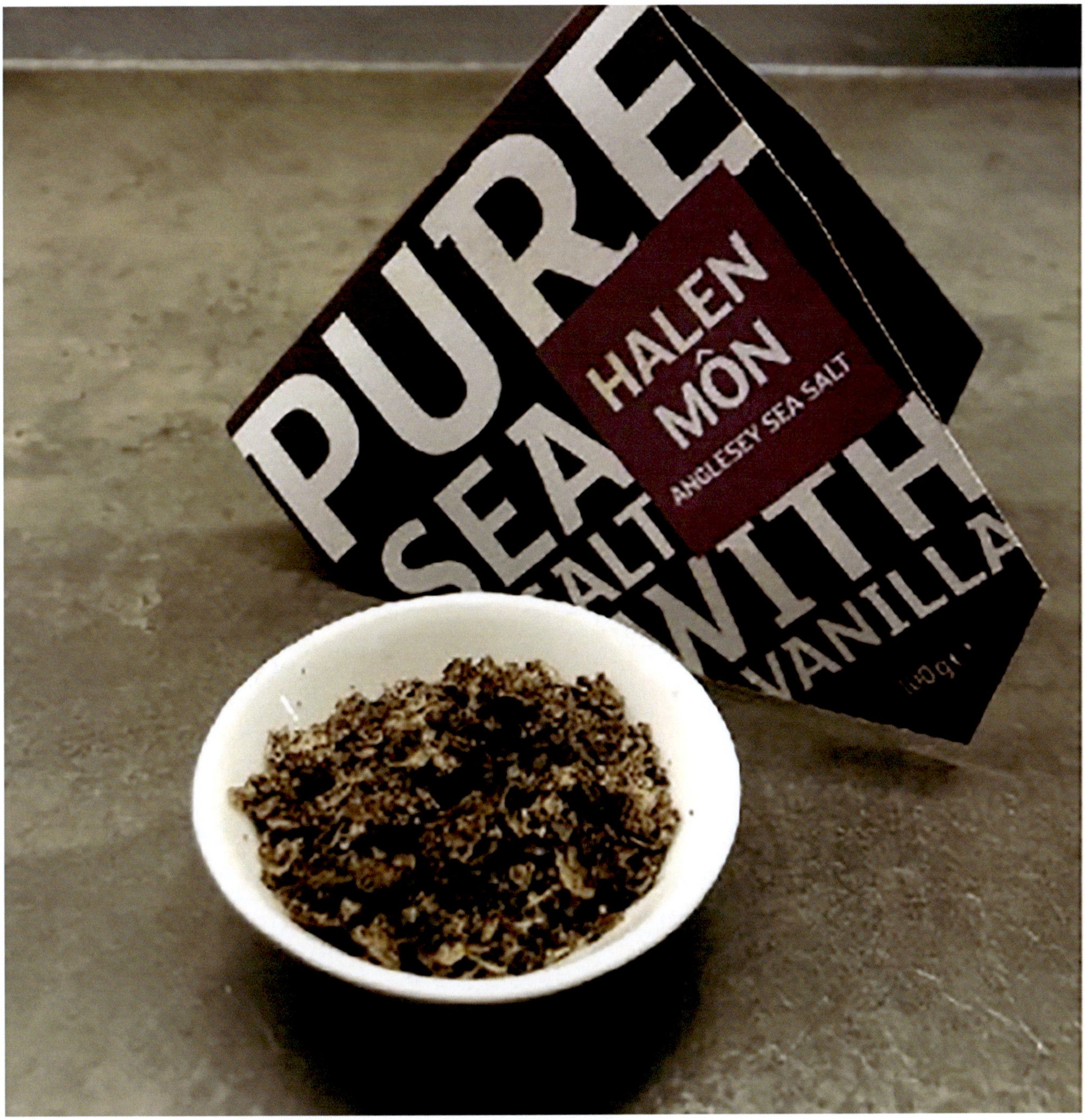
PURE
SEA
WITH
VANILLA
HALEN
MÔN
ANGLESEY SEA SALT

Vanilla bean

Recipe 86

Salzburger Nockerl

An iconic dessert from Salzburg representing the three surrounding hills, the Gaisberg, Mönchsberg, and Kapuzinerberg. The golden tops of this soufflé are dusted with icing sugar to create a snow effect. In the grand dining rooms in Salzburg, happy patrons applaud when this much anticipated dessert arrives.

Dessert
Serves 4
Prep time: 15 minutes
Cooking time 15 to 20 minutes
Gluten-free
Dairy-free

Ingredients

4 eggs, separated
125g/half cup caster sugar
1 pinch salt
30g/1 oz. corn flour
1tbs lemon juice
1 sachet (about a teaspoon) vanilla sugar
Icing/powder sugar for dusting

Method

Preheat oven to 200°C/400°F. Line baking dish with parchment paper/baking paper.

To make the meringue, whip the egg whites with the pinch of salt until fluffy. Slowly add the caster sugar – one teaspoon at a time – and then add the lemon juice while continuing to whip. When the egg whites are super firm, add the corn flour and the 4 egg yolks and blend by hand. Don't over-blend.

Now form mountains of meringue in the baking dish and sprinkle them with vanilla sugar.

Place in the oven and bake for 15 to 20 minutes until the Salzburger Nockerl turns a golden colour and the meringue is stiff.

Remove from oven. Dust with icing/powder sugar and serve immediately. Accompany the dessert with bowls of warm strawberry compôte that has a hint of vanilla.

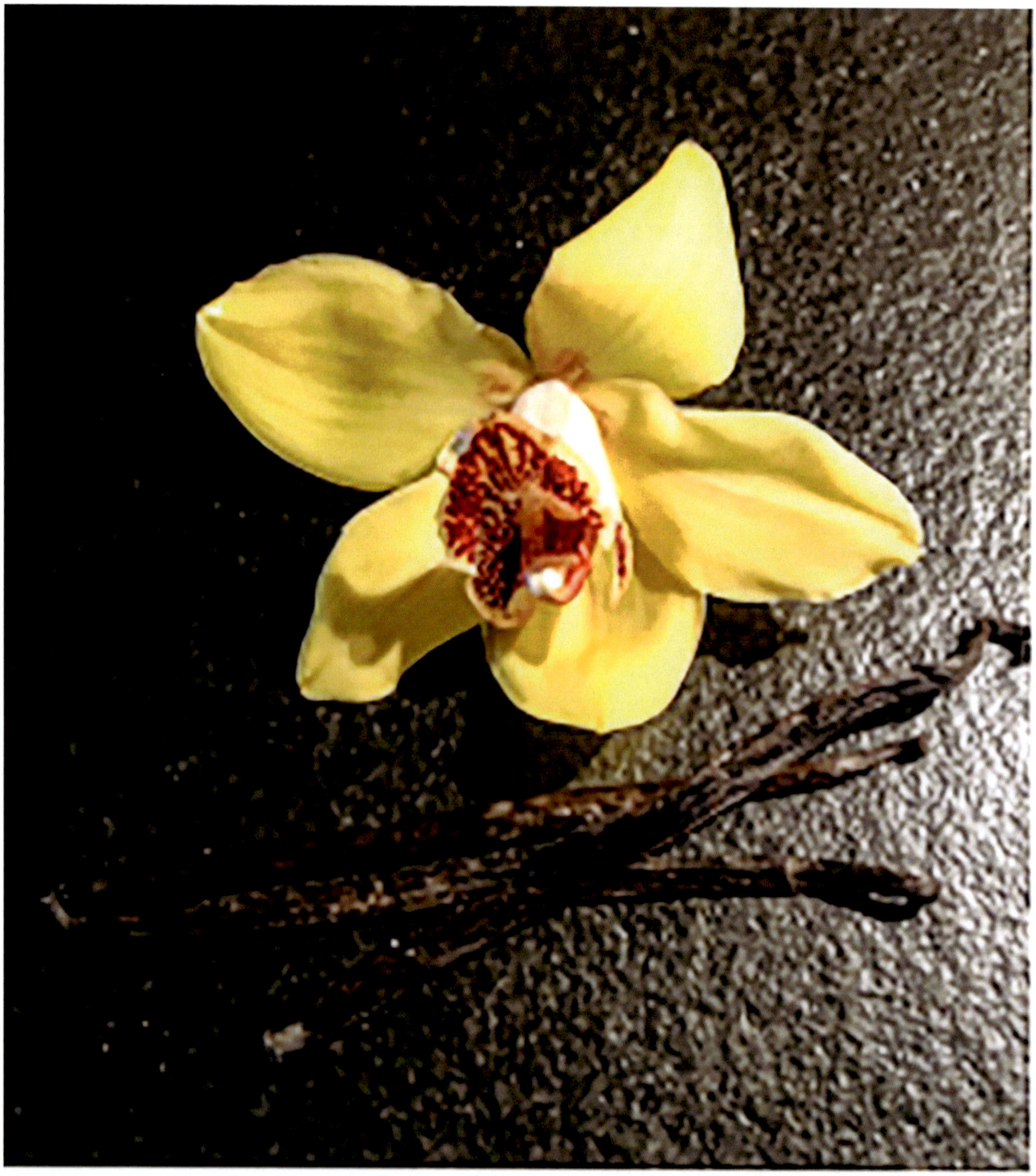

Violette

Recipe 87

Aviation Cocktail

A classic from the golden age of cocktails. A novelty because of its colour and the rarity of crème de violette

Apéro
Serves: 2
Gluten-free
Vegetarian

Ingredients

250ml/8fl oz. gin
2 dashes maraschino liqueur
2 dashes crème de violette
30ml/1fl oz. lemon juice, freshly squeezed
Garnish: lemon peel twist

Method

Pour the gin, liqueurs, and lemon juice into a cocktail-shaker filled with ice.
Shake well until the sides of the shaker become frosty.
Strain into martini glasses.
Garnish with the lemon twist.

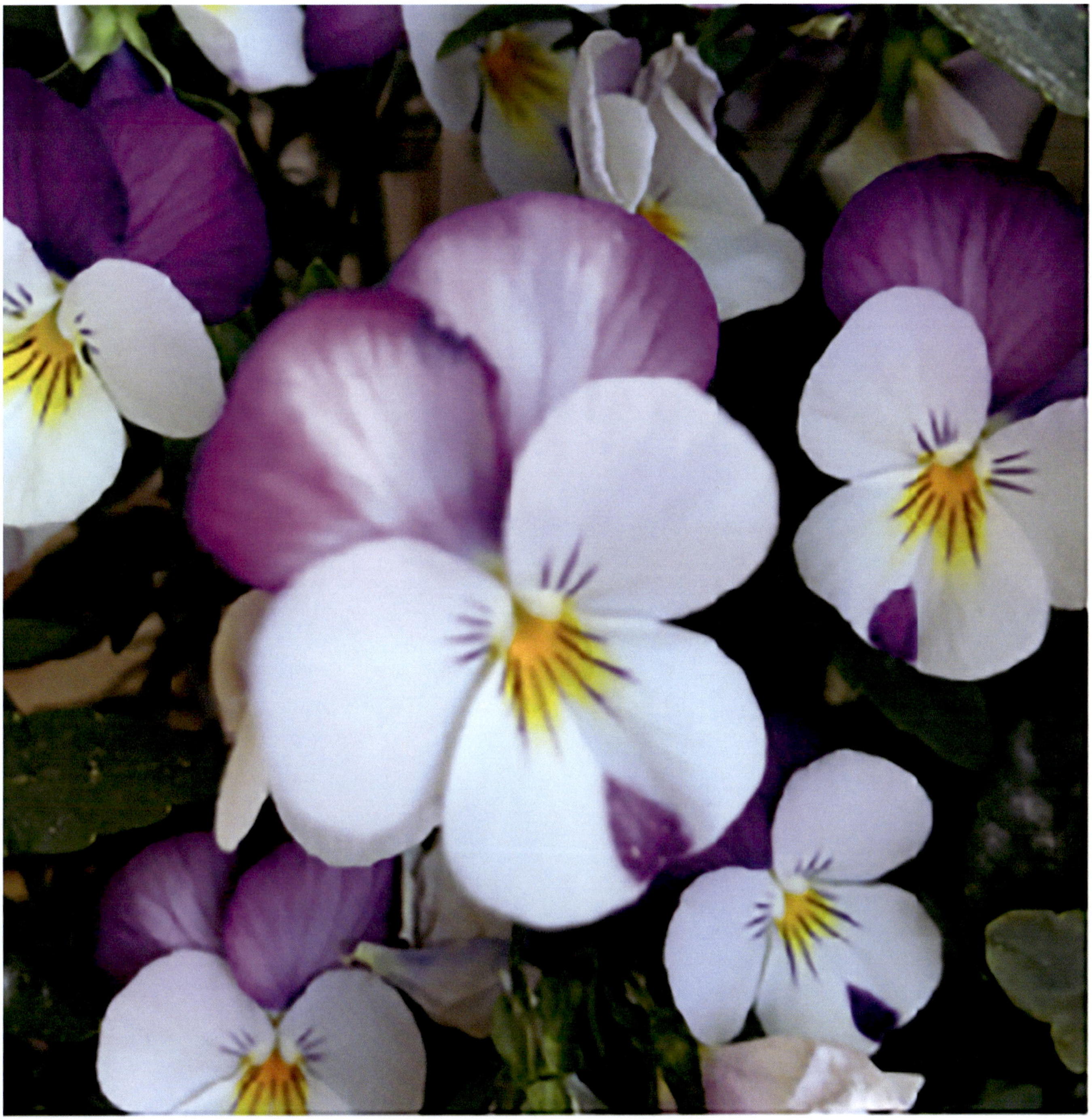

Menu Suggestions

Friends have asked me how to combine some of these 87 recipes into menu suggestions, whether for a three-course meal or for an important celebration.

Saturday Night Dinner for 6

Aviation cocktail: **Recipe 87**

Insalata di pomodori con burrata + basilico: **Recipe 6**

Rosemary focaccia: **Recipe 66**

Perfect roast beef: **Recipe 9**

Sautéed green beans with vanilla salt and butter: **Recipe 85**

Sandra's roasted potatoes: **Recipe 59**

Tiramisu: **Recipe 20**

Wine Suggestion

French Bordeaux or Burgundy

An Indian-Inspired Celebration

Ramos Gin Fizz: **Recipe 54**

Chicken Tikka: **Recipe 32**

with Mango chutney: **Recipe 49**

Piquant potatoes: **Recipe 48**

Grilled aubergine with turmeric, chili, and pomegranate seeds: **Recipe 83**

Butter chicken: **Recipe 29**

Serve with basmati rice.

Tandoori lamb chops: **Recipe 24**

with Raita: **Recipe 50**

Peach crumble with cardamom crust: **Recipe 12**

Wine Suggestions

Italian rosé

Australian merlot

Afternoon Tea

Linden tea: **Recipe 44**

Lavender lemon madeleines: **Recipe 42**

Lemon and poppy seed fairy cakes: **Recipe 63**

A Cold Lunch Buffet

Duchess of Cambridge cocktail: **Recipe 64**

Lemongrass limeade: **Recipe 43**

Gazpacho: **Recipe 14**

Salad Olivieh: **Recipe 77**

Poached peaches with ricotta buttercream and crunchy panko topping: **Recipe 33**

Vitello Tonnato: **Recipe 10**

Moroccan style couscous: **Recipe 23**

Wine Suggestion

Prosecco

Rosé from Provence

Thai Time

Singapore Sling: **Recipe 38**

Moo sarong – pork wrapped in golden threads: **Recipe 34**

with Thai sweet chili sauce: **Recipe 35**

Yam won sen – seafood and cellophane Thai noodle salad: **Recipe 41**

Gaeng pet ped yang – Thai red curry with duck breasts: **Recipe 80**

serve with steamed jasmine rice

Pandam coconut ice cream: **Recipe 58**

or

Orange and pineapple with mint sugar: **Recipe 47**

Wine Suggestion

Chenin blanc from South Africa

Rioja from Spain

A Sunday Lunch

The Remedy – G and T: **Recipe 40**

A Swiss Kiss: **Recipe 37**

Risotto alla Milanese with lemon: **Recipe 69**

Roast rack of lamb: **Recipe 56**

Gratinato di finocchio con noce moscata: **Recipe 52**

Sweet sautéed carrots with orange and marjoram: **Recipe 45**

Forest-fruit claufoutis: **Recipe 17**

Wine Suggestion

Ribolla Gialla

Barolo

Photo : Amanda Douglas

Conversion Tables

Length

1cm	1/2 inch
2.5cm	1 inch
15cm	6 inch
20cm	10 inches
30cm	12 inches

Volume

5ml	1 teaspoon (tsp)	
15ml	1 tablespoon (tbs)	
30ml	1fl oz	1/8 cup
60ml	2fl oz	1/4 cup
75ml		1/3 cup
125ml	4fl oz	1/2 cup
150ml	5fl oz	2/3 cup
175ml		3/4 cup
250ml	8fl oz	1 cup
1 litre	1 quart	4 cups

Weight

25g	1 oz.
50 g	2 oz.
120g	4 oz.
200g	7 oz.
250g	9 oz.
300g	10 oz.
400g	14 oz.
500g	16 oz.
1kg	2lb, 4 oz.

Oven Temperatures

°Celsius	Fahrenheit
140	275
150	300
160	325
180	350
190	375
200	400
220	425
230	450
250	500

Internal Cooking Temperature Guide

Beef

Rare	120°F to 125°F	45°C to 50°C
Medium-rare	130°F to 135°F	55°C to 60°C
Medium	140°F to 145°F	60°C to 65°C
Medium-well	150°F to 155°F	65°C to 70°C
Well-done	160°F and above	70°C and above

Lamb

Rare	135°F	60°C
Medium-rare	140°F to 150°F	60°C to 65°C
Medium	160°F	70°C
Well-done	165°F and above	75°C and above

Chicken	165°F to 175°F	75°C to 80°C
Turkey	165°F to 175°F	75°C to 80°C
Fresh Pork	145°F	63°C
Ham (fully cooked)	140°F	60°C
Ham (uncooked)	145°F	63°C

With Gratitude

Spices of Life and Herbs, Too! has been cooking up in my subconscious for about 10 years and its collection of recipes for over 30. I am grateful to my mother who taught me how to cook. In the kitchen, I remember begging her to let me stir, sift, roll, and flip, and also… to lick the bowl! Over time, she would gently and generously give me more responsibility until one day, the tables turned and it was my pleasure to host the family for Sunday lunches and holiday celebrations.

Thank you to my husband, Gordon, and to my friend, Sandra, who patiently tasted, commented on, researched, edited, and provided invaluable technical support. They gave me courage and kept me smiling. And also to Ulrich of Meticulous Graphics for updating lockedintastes.com and to Mary Ellen for proofreading all of these pages.

Thank you to the market vendors, supermarket staff, butchers, fishmongers, and greengrocers who generously shared tips and recipes and introduced me to some exotic ingredients.

Thank you to the chefs, from starred restaurants to street food vendors, who inspired and shared ideas, techniques, and tastes.

Thank you to my friends and family who, over the years, have accepted lunch and supper invitations. Your enthusiasm, encouragement, and positivity have driven me to try harder, to keep practicing, and to produce a cookbook which includes my most requested recipes.

And to you, my readers, for your curiosity and interest. I wish you the spices of life!

Thank you!